Research Methods
and the New Media

Series in Communication Technology and Society

Everett M. Rogers and *Frederick Williams*, EDITORS

Everett M. Rogers, Communication Technology: The New Media in Society (1986)

Frederick Williams, Ronald E. Rice, and Everett M. Rogers, Research Methods and the New Media (1988)

Robert Johansen, Groupware: Computer Support for Business Teams (1988)

Research Methods and the New Media

Frederick Williams
Ronald E. Rice
Everett M. Rogers

THE FREE PRESS
A Division of Macmillan, Inc.
NEW YORK

Collier Macmillan Publishers
LONDON

The Free Press
A Division of Macmillan, Inc.
866 Third Avenue, New York, N.Y. 10022

Collier Macmillan Canada, Inc.

Printed in the United States of America

printing number
1 2 3 4 5 6 7 8 9 10

Library of Congress Cataloging-in-Publication Data

Williams, Frederick
    Research methods and the new media / Frederick Williams, Ronald E.
Rice, Everett M. Rogers.
        p.   cm—(Series in communication technology and society)
    Bibliography: p.
    Includes index.
    ISBN 0–02–935332–7.   ISBN 0–02–935331–9
    1. Mass media—Research—Methodology.   2. Mass media—
Technological innovations.   I. Rice, Ronald E.   II. Rogers,
Everett M.   III. Title.   IV. Series.
P91.3.W45 1988
001.51′072—dc19   88–11260
                                                          CIP

Page 136: Tables 9–1 and 9–2 from M. Carnoy, "The Economic Costs and Returns to
Educational Television," *Economic Development and Cultural Change*, 28, pp. 237
and 238 (The University of Chicago Press). © 1975 by The University of Chicago.

Page 138: Table 9–3 from I.T. Morita and D.K. Gapen, "A Cost Analysis of The Ohio
State Library Center On-Line Shared Cataloging System in The Ohio State University Libraries," *Library Resources and Technical Services*, 21 (3), 1977, p. 291. By
permission.

*Dedicated to the memory of
Wilbur Schramm,
who influenced us all*

Contents

Preface   xi

PART I. Perspectives on Research on the New Media   1

1. DISTINCTIONS IN THE STUDY OF NEW MEDIA   3
    The New Media   3
    New Media—Components and Combinations   5
        Telecommunications   5
        Computing   7
        New Service Applications   8
    Special Qualities of New Media   10
        Three Dimensions   10
    Some Distinctions of New Media Research   13
    The Research Challenge   14
    Summary   15

2. TRENDS IN THE STUDY OF NEW MEDIA   16
    The Influence of Communication Media on Research   16
    The Media and Research Traditions   17
        The Sequence of Media   17
        Children and Media   19
        Communication Theories and Media   21
    The Direction of Communication Research   23
    Paths Not Taken   25
    Communication Policy Analysis   27
    Expanding the Study of Media Technologies   28
    Summary   30

3. Choosing Among Alternative Research Designs 32
Conflicts Over Research Methods 32
Conventional Approaches 33
  Mathematical Modeling 33
  Controlled Experiments 33
  Quasi-experiments 34
  Surveys 34
  Longitudinal Studies 35
  Field Studies 35
  Archival and Secondary Research 36
  Futures Research and Forecasting 37
  Content Analysis 37
  Case Studies 37
  Focus Groups 38
Assumptions and Criticisms of Conventional and Positivist
  Approaches 38
Alternative to Conventional Research Methods and Designs 41
  Sources and Rationales 41
  Interpretive Approach 43
  Contextualism 43
  Action Research 45
Criteria for Choosing Among Designs and Methods 46
A Triangulation Example in the Study of Word Processing 47
Summary 50
Notes 51

PART II. Problems and Solutions for Research 53

4. Validity, Reliability, and Sampling 55
Requirements of Research Designs 55
A Case Study of Teletext Research 55
Elements of Research Design 58
  Validity 58
  Reliability 61
  Sampling 62
Studying the New Media Over Time 64
  Need for a Temporal Perspective 64
  Choices in Over-time Research 65
  Problems in Studying New Media Over Time 67
Summary 68
Notes 69

5. Adoption of New Media 70
The Importance of Interactivity 70

What Is the Diffusion Paradigm?   70
The Critical Mass in the Adoption of Interactive Media   72
Adoption of Computer-Mediated Communication Systems   75
Implications of the Critical Mass Concept for Research
    Methods   77
Forecasting the Diffusion of New Media   79
    An Emphasis on Prediction   79
    The Failure of Videodisc Players   79
    Centers of Forecasting Research   80
    How Accurate Are Forecasts?   81
    How Is the Rate of Adoption Forecast?   84
    Why Are Certain Forecasting Methods More Accurate?   87
    Can 2 Million French People Be Wrong?   88
Summary   89

6. USING COMPUTER-MONITORED DATA   91
Automating Data Collection   91
Characteristics of Computer-Monitored Data   92
    Advantages for Validity and Reliability   92
    Comparing Computer-Monitored Data to Self-Report
      Data   93
Research Uses of Computer-Monitored Data   94
    Monitoring and Initiating   94
    Types of Data and Research Design Elements   95
    An Example Showing a Combination of Uses   97
    Retesting the Erie County Study with Computer-
      Monitored Surveys   98
Merging Computer-Monitored Data with Questionnaire Data 100
    Data Combinations   100
    Problems   100
    Merging the Data   102
    Results   103
Summary   104

7. STRATEGIES FOR STUDYING CASES   106
Why Do a Case Study?   106
What Defines a Case Study?   106
Microcomputers in the Schools: A Case Study Example   109
    Background and Problem   109
    Method   110
    Results   111
General Steps for Designing a Case Study   113
    1. Specify the Need for a Case Study   113
    2. Define the Unit of Analysis   113

	3. Plan Data-Gathering and Analyses	114
	4. Carry Out the Research Plan	115
	Summary	116
8.	IMPLEMENTING FORMATIVE EVALUATION	117
	A "Developmental" Approach	117
	Characteristics of Formative Evaluation	119
	Background	119
	Evaluation as a Research Focus	120
	Formative as Against Summative Evaluation	121
	Practical Benefits	122
	Uses with New Media	123
	Steps in Formative Evaluation	124
	1. Define Objectives	124
	2. Select the Scope of the Research	125
	3. Select Data-Gathering Methods	126
	4. Analyze Results and Provide Feedback	128
	Formative Evaluation as Mass Communications Research	129
	Summary	130
9.	EVALUATING COSTS AND BENEFITS	131
	Return on Investment	131
	Methods for Costs Analyses	132
	Types of Analyses	132
	Applications to New Media	133
	Major Steps in a Cost Analysis	141
	1. Define the Problem	141
	2. Select the Analysis Method	142
	3. Gather Data	142
	4. Conduct Analysis and Draw Conclusions	143
	Beyond Cost Analyses	143
	Summary	145
10.	MEASURING PRODUCTIVITY	146
	Going Beyond Costs and Benefits	146
	Productivity as Efficiency Ratios	147
	Basic Production Ratios	147
	Ratios of Revenues Relative to Personnel or Technology	149
	Return-on-Investment Ratios	150
	Ratios Relative to Value Added	150
	More on the Value-Added Concept	151
	Examples of Productivity Analyses	153
	Basic Cost-Benefit Analysis	153
	Value Added	154
	Capital-Labor Trade-off	157

New Media as Strategic Investment   157
    Selecting Options   157
    Gaining Competitive Advantage   157
Summary   160

PART III.   **New Considerations**   **161**

11. NEW THEORETICAL APPROACHES   163
The Need for New Theory   163
The Networks and New Media   163
    Network Paradigm, Data, Measures, and Methods   163
    Influence of Networks on Adoption of Computer Systems 166
Interaction and Involvement   169
    The Nature of Interactivity   169
    Psychological Involvement and Interactive Videodiscs 170
    Social Involvement and Parasocial Interaction   173
Summary   174

12. ISSUES OF ETHICS AND IDEOLOGY   176
Human Costs and Benfits   176
Research with Human Subjects   177
    Background   177
    The Belmont Report   178
    Institutional General Assurance   179
    Practical Notes   180
Privacy as an Example of an Ethical Issue   181
    Making Private Information Public   181
    Personal Privacy   183
    Protecting Privacy in Research   185
Equity as an Example of an Ethical Issue   185
Summary   187

Appendix: On-line Data-base Services   **189**

References   **193**

Index   **207**

Preface

Research Methods and the New Media is written for communication scholars who have a special interest in the adoption, implementation, effects, or evaluation of the new communication technologies or in new uses of traditional technologies. The purpose is to bring together under one cover a wide range of methods, strategies, and examples of such research. Our premise in writing this book is that the rapid development and implementation of new media require consideration of innovative research methods for contemporary communication research.

New media are not necessarily replacing older media. Rather, they are supplanting and complementing them by providing otherwise inaccessible or costly communications services. When we use the term "new media" we are refering to technologies of telecommunication and computing, new user devices (e.g., videodisc machines), and their practical applications in office, home, business, health, or educational enviroments. We are concerned with both practical and theoretical research on these new media.

Practical uses for research might include the need to: (1) forecast the likely uses of new media, (2) understand the implementation process, (3) evaluate cost-benefits or productivity of effectiveness, (4) develop policy, and (5) facilitate long-range planing. Some practical examples are assessing cost-benefits of the use of computers in a school setting, or introducing a new "intelligent" telephone system to an organization's users.

Examples of theoretical research include: (1) the process of adoption of new media, (2) the nature of the human-machine interface, (3) the impact of new media on organizational information processing, (4) new roles of media in child socialization, (5) changes in the concept of literacy, (6) the process by which information adds value to other activities, and (7) changes in the nature of work. Theoretical studies have a deeper concern for the fundamental variables affecting usage and interpretations of new media, and, in particular, intermediate and long-range effects. Thus, for example, the role of computer-mediated communication systems in designing organizations is a theoretical issue, as is the longer range effects of new entertainment media on children.

Although three of us have developed this book, we have very much attempted to present the material from a "single-author" perspective, both in the design of chapters as well as in their style. To accomplish this, we have each participated in the development of all chapters of the book, and we therefore hold ourselves equally responsible for the strengths and weaknesses of what is presented in the volume. Because we are preparing this book during a period we believe precedes a substantial growth in the implementaion and evaluation of new media, we hope you will share your reactions with us.

F.W.
R.E.R.
E.M.R.

PART I

Perspectives on Research on the New Media

CHAPTER 1

Distinctions in the Study of New Media

The New Media

One mark of communication research of the last twenty or so years has been the growth of interest in the adoption, implementation, and effects of new communication technologies, and in new versions of older technologies. Of course, "technology" itself is not a new concept to human communication. It relates distantly even to those tools our ancestors used to expand their communications beyond their naturally endowed capabilities. The stones our ancestors used to scratch their marks on rocks, the fires they used for signaling, or the sticks they used for counting were all early technologies of a sort. More advanced tools, and more technological inventions, were writing, the printing press, papermaking, the telegraph, photography, the telephone, and broadcasting. Indeed, much of the history of human communication is marked by the "science of the practical"— that is, the uses of technologies to extend our communication capabilities.

When we refer in this book to the "new media," we mainly mean those media technologies, mostly electronic and digital, that are undergoing expansion in our times. The key technologies underlying the new media include microelectronics, computers, and telecommunications networks. A medium might be as singularly "new" as interactive videodiscs, yet there are many examples where "new" represents an extension of an older medium—for example, the computer-switched telephone network, the teletext system that uses part of a television signal, and the teleconferencing system that mixes voice, data, and image. Table 1–1 provides a summary of many of the traditional levels of communications and their expansion through new media.

As shown in Table 1–1, the new media facilitate all levels—from intrapersonal to mass—of the communication process. Technologies such as microelectronics expand the capabilities of existing commu-

Table 1–1. Applications of Technologies to Different Levels of Communication

Type of Communication	Traditional Technologies	Recent Innovations
Intrapersonal	Notes to self, diary, photographs, self-monitored feedback, calculators	Audio- or videotape, computer programming, problem-solving with a computer
Interpersonal	"Point-to-point" mail, telephone, telegraph, copying machines	Facsimile, computer communications, electronic mail, mobile telephone, paging devices, personal videotaping
Group (point-to-point)	"Telephone conferences"	Teleconferencing with full audio and visual links, computer conferencing, electronic chalkboards
Large group	Microphones, slide or overhead projector, motion pictures	Videoprojection, audience polling systems
Organizational	Memos, telephone, intercom	Management information system, computer time-sharing, facsimile, teleconferencing, personal computing, word processing, electronic mail
Mass	Newspaper, radio, television, films, magazines, books, billboards	Cable and pay TV, video and teletext, videotape, video- or audio disc, portable radio and tape players (e.g., Sony "Walkman"), videogames, interactive TV, public information and computing networks, data radio

nications systems, often making these systems less expensive, more reliable, more portable, and allowing content to be more independent of physical contact than such traditional channels as letters or face-to-face conversations. Computer technologies allow users to process communication by altering the structure of interactions and by editing, storing, and retrieving content. Telecommunications networks allow users in diverse locations to communicate with each other and to expand their social structure to include others whom they had not known before.

These new capabilities allow for changes in human communication behaviors on intra- and inter-personal levels, in groups, organizations, and in mass audience contexts. They raise questions about the potential of new media, about how they are adopted and implemented, what their effects may be in both immediate and long-range contexts, and, above all, about the larger social questions concerning their benefits to humanity. It is therefore important that we expand our capabilities for studying the new media just as the technologies themselves have expanded.

In this first chapter, we discuss major distinctions of new media and associated distinctions of research in this area.

New Media—Components and Combinations

TELECOMMUNICATIONS

One major area of development is in the transmission of human messages through telecommunications systems. These technologies are, either singularly or as a part of other systems, contributing to new possibilities for human interaction. Some are newer than others, but all are currently an important part of new media.

Optical transmission systems involve the modulation of light waves as a communications carrier. Two common forms are the highly focused "laser" beams and the optical fibers that serve as communications channels. Optical systems have the potential to be far less expensive than traditional telecommunications systems. They have a large signal capacity and are freer of interference than electrical or electronic systems. Much of the planned expansion of the public switched (telephone) network will use optical fiber technology.

Communications satellites are broadcast relay stations that, because of their position above the earth, can disseminate signals over a wider area than a land-based station. When in an orbit matching the movement of the earth's surface (called a "geosynchronous" orbit), earth stations can easily "lock on" to the satellite and need not incorporate expensive tracking mechanisms. As satellites become able to broadcast increasingly powerful signals, earth stations can be reduced in size, making satellite communication much less expensive and more widely available.

Coaxial cable allows for the simultaneous transmission of many individual messages, including moving video images, which require large bandwidths. Cable is known for its application in the distribution of television signals to homes. However, modern cable has many enhancements; these include two-way or interactive transmission; simultaneous delivery of voice, data, and images; and applications ranging from security systems to remote reading of home electric or gas meters.

Microwave relay systems allow for the line-of-sight transmission of many simultaneous voice, data, and image signals from tower to tower. As a substitute for wired telecommunication systems, these relay stations have greatly reduced the cost of building telecommunications networks.

Cellular mobile telecommunication systems include a network of low-power broadcast grids where every cell has a different frequency so that many callers can share the overall network. As callers travel from one cell to another, their communication channel is automatically shifted to one of the different frequencies.

Local area networks are dedicated communication networks often used to link individuals in a building, buildings in a complex, or the geographically separated units of a single company or organization. These networks typically bypass the local telephone network. A major application is an integrated communication network in modern office buildings, a system sometimes referred to as "shared tenant services."

Value-added common carrier networks use various combinations of the preceding transmission channels to provide reliable, less-expensive telecommunications service. "Value added" refers to the offering of processing capabilities such as storage and forwarding of messages at a later time, least-cost routing, error-checking, and detailed accounting records. A particularly significant characteristic of such networks is their use of packet-switching, which breaks up a message into small packets; sends each one along the fastest, cheapest, or most reliable route; and reassembles the packets at the destination computer.

One of the most important contemporary trends in telecommunications is the digitalization of signals. When in digital form, signals can transfer voice, data, and image information easily in the same network. Digital signals can include their own "routing" instructions. There is a move toward a world standard in digital networks; this standard is called the integrated systems digital network—ISDN for short.

COMPUTING

The computer is as much a communication technology as it is computational in that it facilitates the movement, storage, and reproduction of messages. But whereas communication technologies typically only change the energy form of messages for purposes of transmission, computers can change the messages themselves. In this respect we can think of a computer receiving messages as "programs" to act on other messages as "data." But even more applicable to communication research is that computers are integral parts of most modern telecommunications systems. Some of the world's most sophisticated computers serve as "switches" for major communications networks. Moreover, miniaturized computerlike components enable the operation of most transmission and receiver technologies, ranging from telephones to television sets.

Some contemporary computer concepts and designs are as follows:

Microprocessors integrate all the circuits necessary for the basic computing operation on one miniature medium, which is called a chip. These chips are the basis for computerized functions in various types of equipment, such as those mentioned above. When microprocessors are combined with data input-output and memory devices, the combination represents the essentials of a microcomputer.

Personal computers are the popular models of microcomputers now found in homes, schools, and offices, often selling for under $5,000. Currently, they are single-user-oriented, but they are increasingly being designed for simultaneous multiple users and multiple tasks.

Minicomputers have a greater computation capacity and speed than personal computers, can often run several programs simultaneously, and serve multiple users connected through multiple terminals attached to a local area or value-added network. Minicomputers sell in the $10,000 to $500,000 range.

Mainframe computers are the traditional computers found in large installations and originally affordable only by large businesses, government, and the military. These computers serve many simultaneous users ("time-sharing") and usually cost millions of dollars. Many of the capabilities of the older mainframes are now provided by minicomputers.

Supercomputers are the high-speed mainframe computers originally used for military and scientific purposes but are now coming into wider use in business and design applications. They are the most expensive of the computer types.

Artificial intelligence (AI) is the creation of program materials that reflect human intellectual capabilities for learning, reasoning, adapting, guessing, and simulating. AI has led to advances in robotics, vision, language processing, and decision making. Some communications applications include the design of large networks, monitoring communications satellites, engineering design, online information systems that "learn" from a user's prior searches, and motion picture animation.

NEW SERVICE APPLICATIONS

Rather than considering specific examples of telecommunications, computing, or combined systems, we often consider new media in terms of a particular type of service. Some examples include the following:

Teleconferencing is a meeting of three or more people in two or more separate locations held via interactive electronic communication. Three main types of teleconferencing are video teleconferencing, audio conferencing, and computer conferencing.

Teletext is an information service that allows individuals to request frames of information for viewing on a home television screen. The frames are transmitted in the vertical blanking interval of a conventional television broadcast signal, and the "lines" of information for teletext are located above the picture visible on the television set. Each of the several hundred frames that are broadcast in an ongoing cycle of broadcasts can be chosen by an individual via a keypad and, after decoding, viewed on a television set.

Videotext is an interactive information service that allows individuals to request frames of information from a central computer for viewing on a video display screen. The number of frames or lines of information is limited only by the capacity of the computer in the videotext system. Videotext requires a request channel (unlike teletext), so it is much more interactive in nature. The most common and accessible form of videotext is the online data-base, containing bibliographic materials, trend data from historical data-bases, full text of articles, the latest news, and much more.

Interactive cable television provides the ability to send text and graphic frames, as well as full video pictures, to home television sets via cable in answer to requests that the viewer enters on a keypad. The diversity of content is potentially unlimited. The cable typically serves as the request channel as well as the conduit for the requested information or programs, although some hybrid systems use telephone lines. The source computer is usually capable of polling and tabulating responses and accepting orders for services or products.

Computer-mediated communication systems consist of a main computer that stores and processes message content; it is connected to users by telecommunications networks. Two main types of computer-mediated communication systems are electronic messaging and computer conferencing (of which computer bulletin boards are a simpler, more nonprofit form). The users of an electronic messaging system typically belong to a single organization. In contrast, the users of a computer conference are often at scattered locations with their terminals linked by a wired network, including those provided by telephone companies.

High-definition television is a system that increases the scanning lines over the current U.S. standard of 525 lines, or the European standard of 625 lines, to up to 2,000 lines. This change provides a much clearer and detailed image. Such images lend themselves to many applications, such as computer-aided-design, instructional and scientific systems, image processing, or simply a high-quality image for home entertainment (including large-screen displays).

Low-powered television allows for television stations with a small broadcasting radii, which would result in more alternative stations. Ideally, this form of television could lead to the development of neighborhood broadcast stations, a trend away from the "mass" orientation of traditional television.

Special Qualities of New Media

THREE DIMENSIONS

Although the new media share many characteristics with traditional media, there are distinctions that suggest possible implications for human communication. As the basis for examples, we will briefly discuss three such qualities: interactivity, de-massification, and asynchroneity. These qualities are defined below; their distinctions among traditional communication channels are summarized in Table 1–2.

Interactivity

The degree to which participants in a communication process have control over, and can exchange roles in, their mutual discourse is called interactivity. By *mutual discourse*, we mean the degree to which a given communication act is based on a prior series of communication acts. Bretz (1983) proposes that a high degree of interactivity implies a third-order dependency: A's response to B depends on B's

Table 1–2. Some Distinctions Among Interpersonal, Interactive, and Mass Media Communication Channels

Characteristics of Communication Channels	Face-to-face Interpersonal Communication	Interactive Communication	Mass Media
Flows	One-to-few	Many-to-many	One-to-many
1. Degree of de-massification	High	High	Low (the same message is transmitted to everyone)
2. Degree of interactivity	High	High	Low
3. Asynchroneity	Low	High for most types of the new media	Low, but high for some media, such as books and news-papers

SOURCE: Based on Rogers (1986, p. 21). See also Rice (1987b) for a more detailed discussion of media characteristics.

prior response to A's initial communication acts. By *exchange of roles*, we mean the ability of individual A to take the position of individual B and thus to perform B's communication acts, and vice versa. In the example of a third-order interaction, both A and B are respondents to the other's communication, so they are fully able to exchange roles. By having *control*, we mean the extent to which an individual can choose the timing, content, and sequence of a communication act, search out alternative choices, enter content into the storage for other users, and perhaps create new system capabilities. By *participants*, we mean at least one individual communicating with at least one source of information, or two or more individuals using a common medium. We call them participants instead of sources and receivers because of their coequal roles in exchanging information and constructing meaning.

Using the concepts of mutual discourse, exchange, control, and participants, we can compare the degree of interactivity in a videotext system and a teletext system. A teletext system, B, broadcasts a stream of several hundred pages of information, and the user, A, responds by selecting one or more of these pages to display on a television screen. Because there is no two-way link in a teletext system, there is no possibility for an exchange of roles (i.e., the user does not send any information to add to the content of the system), so the level of discourse is only second-order. However, the user has considerable control over the timing, content, and sequencing of these pages. In some teletext systems, the user can store these pages for later use, thus extending the degree of control. Participation is limited to a communication process between the user and the system (which makes the pages accessible from a data-base of pages) rather than directly between individuals. However, the user does communicate with the wider system of data-collectors, data-entry personnel, system and page designers, and vendors, to name a few.

Now consider the degree of interactivity in a videotext system. Because there is a two-way link between the user and the videotext data-base, there is the possibility for an exchange of roles to a certain degree. Whether roles can be exchanged is a matter of debate. The distinguishing criterion may be whether the "communication act" must involve cognition by all participants. If that is the criterion, no communication with a nonhuman participant is truly interactive. One perspective is that the information available is just as fixed during a particular videotext communication session as in a teletext session, so roles cannot really be exchanged—that is, the videotext system cannot take the user's role and conduct original searches for information. However, it can be programmed to conduct the same search on new or more recent sets of information, and, with artificial intelligence, it can be programmed to learn from how the user makes requests and from what sets of information are requested.

A different perspective argues that because later sets of information are dependent on the user's response to prior sets of information, a third-order relation exists. However, it is clear that the user has considerably more control with videotext than with teletext not only because of the far greater amount of content available, but also because of the ability to revise continuously the kinds and amount of content communicated. Because of their two-way link, most videotext systems also allow participants to exchange messages with other participants, further extending the degree of interactivity experienced in using this new medium.

Face-to-face discussions are generally felt to have the greatest degree of interactivity because of their potential for fulfilling the conditions of mutual discourse, exchange of roles, user control, and participation. However, note that there are many situations in which one or all of these conditions are not met in an actual conversation. An extreme case of a military recruit in boot camp standing in front of the drill instructor suggests that social conditions can remove most of the potential for interactivity in a face-to-face communication situation. Further, some new media offer even a greater degree of control by the user than are possible in face-to-face conversations. For example, interactive videodiscs (Chapter 11) designed for educational purposes can provide the student with greater access to, and control of, visual, audio, and textual content than can a classroom teacher.

Perhaps our present examples emphasize what is fundamental to determinations of interactivity in any medium. The users' social situation and the nature of the communication process are the primary determinants of the degree of interactivity, as well as the characteristics and capabilities of a particular technology.

De-massification

To the degree that a special message can be obtained by each individual in a large audience, the new media are also *de-massifying*. Such individualization likens the new media to face-to-face interpersonal communication (except that they are not face-to-face). The potential de-massification of the new media means that they are, in this respect at least, unlike mass media. De-massification means that a certain degree of the control of mass communication systems moves from the message producer to the media consumer. The reader of a newspaper like *The Sunday New York Times* also has a type of control in choosing to read certain news items and ignoring the rest.

Asynchroneity

The new communication technologies are also *asynchronous*, meaning they allow for the sending and receiving of messages at a time convenient for the individual user rather than requiring all participants to use the system at the same time. For example, say an electronic message is sent to you on a value-added computer network. You may receive it on your home or office computer whenever you log on the host computer. Unlike a telephone call, electronic messaging systems avoid the problem of "telephone tag" that occurs when you call someone who is unavailable, and they return your call when you are unavailable. But, of course, the new media cannot guarantee that the intended receiver will ever read the message or respond to it.

Some Distinctions of New Media Research

New media research does not necessarily reflect new methods for research nor an entirely different focus from traditional media research. For one, as we discuss in Chapter 2, the media of communication have long been a focus for research, including such technologies as film, radio, or television in their times. What we do point out, however, is that some of the distinctions of new, and especially interactive, media raise new challenges for research. The new media are extending the dissemination, interaction, or consequences of human communication. We suggest that one task of communication researchers is to understand these distinctions.

As for methodology, we take the position (Chapter 3) that the new media researcher should understand and take advantage of alternative research designs, including use where appropriate of multiple research methods or "triangulation." Accordingly, we examine briefly a variety of methods as they may apply to new media research, including, for example, mathematical modeling, controlled experiments, quasi-experiments, surveys, longitudinal studies, field stud-

ies, archival and secondary research, futures research and forecasting, content analysis, case studies, and focus groups. We also
suggest the consideration of alternatives to conventional research
methods and designs as found in critical or interpretive approaches.

Much of this volume, then, focuses on those special considerations of the study of new media that should allow us to evaluate new
media and their applications with equally innovative research strategies. As with developments in the media, these research approaches
are more extensions than replacements of traditional research
methods.

The Research Challenge

Most of the aforementioned qualities of new communication technologies have the potential to change the way we adopt, implement, or
react to new media. Also, we can see how many new media open
options for changing the environment for communication. For example, do group processes change when participants in a meeting use
teleconferencing rather than interact face-to-face? What are the effects of thirty to fifty channels of cable television, videocassettes,
teletext, or high-definition displays? Will they increase the amount of
time viewers spend watching television, the type of television programming, or cultural and political consequences of that content?
Computers have vastly increased the capability of storing personal
information about citizens, increasing the possibility that government
and educational, health care, and business organizations will share
this information. What are the dangers in this? Should there be new
laws regarding privacy and access to data? Do citizens deserve the
right of free access to data or exchange as they do free speech? And
then there is the equity issue: To what degree are *all* citizens benefit-
ing from the new communication technologies? Are we moving into a
society where most citizens will have greater opportunities for information and expression with the new technologies? Or are we moving
into an era of increased social stratification—the information rich
versus the information poor?

These are the types of questions that intrigue researchers of the
new media. They range from the study of individual people interacting with specific technologies to a broad inquiry of the consequences
of these new media in different societies.

Summary

In this book, we consider the new media as those media technologies, mostly electronic and digital, that are growing in use in our times. The new media themselves consist primarily of combinations of tele-communications, computing, and user devices. These underlie such new media services as teleconferencing, teletext and videotext, interactive cable television, and computer-mediated communication to name a few.

We suggest that many new media have special qualities important to consider in research. These include interactivity, or the exchange of communicators' roles in an exchange; de-massification, or the quality of personalized messages as against mass-oriented ones; and asynchroneity, or the ability to exchange messages at times convenient to the individual users of a communication system.

Finally, although we consider possible research methods for new media as mainly extensions of existing methods, we propose that the new media researcher should consider alternative methods, or even multiple methods, and to attempt a triangulation of methods.

CHAPTER 2

Trends in the Study of New Media

The Influence of Communication Media on Research

Considering communication research has been around for over four decades, it is strange that more attention has not been paid to the intellectual history of this field. Only rare and partial accounts of the history are available—examples are Rowland (1982), Czitrom (1982), Schramm (1985), Wartella and Reeves (1985), Rogers (1986), and Reardon (1987). However, the appearance of these histories of communication research in recent years shows a growing academic interest on the part of communication scholars in knowing their roots. A key element in this history is the role of communication media.

How have communication media influenced research over the decades? In this chapter we trace the trends that emerge in communication research from around 1900 to the present. Our analysis of how the agenda for communication research was set shows that the intellectual concerns of the field were heavily influenced by each of the new communication media as they came on the American scene—including newspapers, film, radio, television, and, now, interactive media. The influence of succeeding waves of communication media on the ensuing communication research may be at least as important in explaining the discipline's history as the rise, fall, and rise of belief in the power of communication effects (a historical simplification that has been widely used by mass communication scholars to delineate eras in communication research). Certainly "the scientific problems that are investigated . . . are heavily influenced by the times in which the knowledge is sought" (Lowery & DeFleur, 1983, p. xi). A new communication medium attracts the attention of some communication scholars the way a lightning rod draws electricity.

The Media and Research Traditions

THE SEQUENCE OF MEDIA

In the early part of this century, newspapers were the dominant mass medium in the United States. Such scholars as John Dewey and Robert E. Park at the University of Chicago, who acted as the roots of communication research, mainly theorized about, and conducted research on, newspapers. They investigated the actual and potential effects of newspapers in ameliorating or exacerbating the important social problems of the American society of their day. These early scholars mainly used qualitative methods, abhorring statistics.

When film began to command large national audiences in the 1920s and 1930s, coordinated programs of research such as the Payne Fund studies were launched to determine the possibly harmful effects of film-viewing on children and youth. The Payne Fund research program consisted of a series of thirteen studies published from 1929 to 1932. These investigations "were the great pioneering effort that established media research as a serious scientific field" (Lowery & DeFleur, 1983, p. 54). The Payne Fund research showed that American children went to the movies about once a week, and that 72 percent of the 500 feature films appearing in 1920, 1925, and 1930 dealt with the themes of crime, sex, and love (Lowery & DeFleur, 1983). Understandably, parents were concerned about the effects of this new technology on their children, and this fit well with the intellectual curiosity of social scientists studying media effects.

Mass communication research first developed in the 1930s because until then the social sciences had not matured to the point at which investigators could seriously attack the intellectual issue of media effects. Statistical methods, more precise measurement techniques (L. L. Thurstone's attitude scale construction research was a Payne Fund study), and the eventual trend toward using computers all marked the development of social science research as it moved toward empirical, quantitative investigation. "It was not until these research tools began to be available that a scientific approach to the study of mass communication could get its start" (Lowery & DeFleur, 1983, p. 21).

In the 1930s, radio became an important new mass medium in the United States, and Paul F. Lazarsfeld saw it as a major topic for communication research. He played an important methodological role in improving the research techniques and designs used by communication scholars to investigate media effects: content analysis, survey interviews, panel designs, and multivariate data-analysis. Further, Lazarsfeld founded an institute at Columbia University that specialized in conducting communication research, originally on the effects of radio, but later on other communication topics as well. His radio research was sponsored by the Rockefeller Foundation and, later, by CBS and other media industries. Thus, Lazarsfeld was a pioneer in launching the university-based research institute, an idea that was followed by other social scientists at various universities.

Wilbur Schramm founded such an institute for communication research at the University of Illinois in 1947 and at Stanford University in 1956. The first Ph.D. students in mass communication were taught at the Institute of Communications Research at Illinois during the 1950s, thus launching the first graduate training in this new field. At this time, television was spreading to most households in the United States; Schramm and his colleagues conducted some of the first research on television's effects on children. In the 1960s, considerable attention was paid to the uses of television as an instructional technique. In the next three decades, several thousand studies of the effects of television were conducted in the United States.

The first uses of computers (in the 1950s and 1960s) by social scientists were for data-analysis and, somewhat later, as teaching machines. This was the era of expensive mainframe computers, which were often accessed by users on a time-sharing basis through remote terminals. Gradually it was realized that these dispersed users could utilize their terminals to communicate with each other through the central computer. In the late 1970s, microcomputers began to replace the mainframes for many purposes, including that of computer-based communication. A growing number of communication scientists in the 1980s conduct research on the social impacts of new interactive media, most of which contain a computer element. A recent survey of faculty, based upon questionnaires sent to a random sample of 200 universities with mass communication or communication technology departments, suggests (1) that cable television is the most frequently researched of the new media (indicated by 40 percent of the respondents), followed by satellite distribution systems (26 percent); and videotext (26 percent); (2) that social issues are the most frequently considered aspects of new media (34 percent), followed by legal and regulatory issues (31 percent); and (3) that the most frequently used methods were legal/historical (53 percent), surveys (44 percent), and interviews (32 percent), although most researchers used a combination of quantitative and qualitative methods (Christy, 1988). Judging from such indicators as the titles of papers presented at the International Communication Association in the 1980s, the study of the new media has become an important concern of communication scholars (Rice & Associates, 1984, Chapter 1), just as prior researchers have studied the "new" media of their eras.

CHILDREN AND MEDIA

Children have often been the subject of media research. Here, many communication scholars implicitly seem to have been strong technological determinists, assuming that new communication technologies are one of the important causes of changes in society. Attention has been given to children and youth as an audience for possible negative effects because younger people are more accepting of each new technology and less prepared to evaluate their use of media than are adults, and thus are a priority audience for assessing the social impacts of new media. In the past, children have served as a kind of litmus paper for the initial studies of the effects of film, television, and computers.

Wartella and Reeves (1985), from their review of research literature on children and mass media communication, concluded: "With the development of each modern means of storytelling—books, newspapers, movies, radio, comics, and television—social debates regarding their effects have recurred. A prominent theme in all these debates has been a concern with media's impact on youth." Further, Wartella and Reeves concluded that "The origin of research about children lies in concern expressed by the public about each medium as it was introduced. Public debate helped shape research agendas— at least with respect to topics—rather than research shaping public concerns or policy." Finally, the authors found that for each of their three media of study (film, radio, and television), the first communication research typically dealt with *use* ("Which children use television? How much?"), which then gave way in a few years to research on the medium's potentially harmful effects on children (typically dealing with violence, sex, and advertising).

Figure 2–1 shows Wartella and Reeves's findings on the relationship between the number of communication research publications per year and consumer adoption of film, radio, and television. Research on children and the mass media has not been cumulative. Across the decades, a new medium (say film) would become the focus of investigation only to be dropped as scientific attention turned to a yet newer medium (e.g., radio). Successive waves of research have thus occurred, with each wave cresting on a new communication medium. Note that the rate of consumer adoption of film, radio, and television had not decreased when the scholars moved on to their next new medium of study.

Television research on children started slowly, with only 300 publications (in English) appearing before 1970, and then speeded up

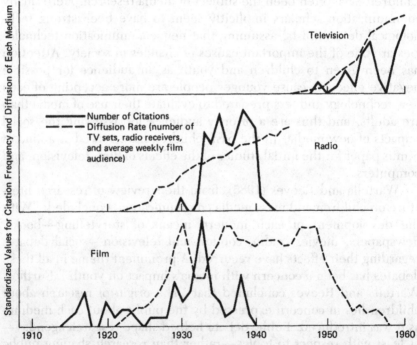

Figure 2–1. Number of Citations about Media and Youth by Diffusion Rate for Film, Radio, and Television, 1910–60

SOURCE: Ellen Wartella and Byron Reeves, "Historical Trends in Research on Children and the Media: 1900–1960." From the *Journal of Communication*, 1985; 35(2):126. © 1985 *Journal of Communication*. Reprinted by permission.

tremendously, with about 830 publications on this topic between 1970 and 1975, and 1,670 in 1976 to 1980 (Chen, 1984, p. 278). The two most extensively researched topics were the effects of television violence on children's aggressive behavior, and the social world portrayed on television and children's socialization (for example, the effects of TV advertising on children's socialization as consumers). Scholarly interest in television effects was undoubtedly encouraged by the millions of dollars of research funds provided through the U.S. Surgeon General's Committee on Television and Social Behavior in the late 1960s. Chen (1984, p. 277) concluded: "To date, television has been the most closely studied communication medium; children have been its most highly researched audience."

If past scholarly experiences with film, radio, and television technologies are repeated in the contemporary era with new media, communication scholars will first investigate the uses of computers by children. The focus may then shift to potential negative effects. Eventually, after such research has run its course, communication scholars will shift their attention to an even newer medium.

COMMUNICATION THEORIES AND MEDIA

Communication research could not really get under way as an academic enterprise until it had a theoretical paradigm to provide direction. A paradigm is a scientific approach to a phenomenon that provides model problems and solutions to a community of scholars. The influential paradigm for communication scholars was provided by Claude Shannon's information theory (Shannon & Weaver, 1949), which was translated and simplified by social scientists of communication to fit with their research on communication effects.

Shannon, a Ph.D. in electrical enringeering, proposed a theory of signal transmission from a source to a destination. His theory was stated in general terms, and it seemed as if his model would apply to any type of human communication. The key concept in Shannon's theory was information, which he proposed to be measured in bits (for "binary digits," as each bit can have two values, "0" or "1"). Information is quantified by determining its value based on what it contributes to prior knowledge. In order to constitute information, a message must reduce uncertainty. A message that conveys information makes the choice among alternative actions easier. Shannon's communication model led to a series of theoretical propositions about the conditions affecting the rate of transmission of information. Each proposition was stated in a precise mathematical expression. This formulation was the basis for tremendous advances in the design of electronic communication systems.

When he proposed his mathematical theory of communication in 1948, Shannon reflected the communication technology of his day. Telegraph and radio were widely used, television was in its early stage of diffusion to U.S. households, and most Americans used the telephone. Shannon worked for Bell Labs, the research and development (R&D) unit of AT&T, the giant telephone company. Understandably, Shannon proposed a theory of electrical signal transmission applicable to one-way communication systems, and feedback was not an important part of it. Shannon's signal transmission theory was a product of its time, including the electrical communications media of its time. Social scientists then tried to apply Shannon's theory to a wide range of communication behaviors, a broadening that led to a bias toward a one-way, linear view of the communications process, and that may have led the field of communication research away from more fruitful directions. However, Shannon did not concern himself with the subjective meaning that a receiver gives to a message, which is usually different from the meaning intended when the message was formed (or from the message content that is communicated).

An alternative paradigm available at the same time as Shannon's theory, Norbert Wiener's (1948) cybernetic model of a communication system, was largely ignored by early communication scholars because it did not fit well with the one-way media (of newspapers, film, and radio) then dominant, or with the effects-orientation of communication researchers. Wiener was a professor of mathematics at MIT who worked on research to improve the accuracy of antiaircraft fire during World War II. He approached this problem with a mathematical model of feedback in which each shell fired was considered a message. The degree to which it approached a target was then information to be fed back to the electronic gunsight of the antiaircraft gun so that the next shot (fired a few seconds later) would be more accurate. After the war, Wiener popularized his cybernetic theory of self-regulating systems in his best-selling books, *Cybernetics* (1948) and *The Human Use of Human Beings* (1950). His theory rapidly became popular as biologists, psychiatrists, engineers, and others applied cybernetic theory to problems in their fields. Some communication scholars became followers of Wiener's, and the concept of feedback was incorporated into models of human communication. But since only limited types of feedback occur with the one-way mass media of the press and broadcasting, the intellectual impact of Wiener's cybernetic theory was more limited than Shannon's linear model.

However, a resurgence of academic interest in Wiener's cybernetic theory is occurring because it corresponds with the interactive nature of many of the new media, as discussed in Chapter 1. The interactivity of the new media makes cybernetic theories of human communication more appropriate to the study of new media than are linear theories (Chapter 11).

This brief history of media and of communication theories suggests several factors that have affected the general directions taken by communication research in the United States:

- The nature of each communication medium as it came on the American scene (e.g., film, radio, television, and computers)
- The concerns of society about communication (e.g., parents' fears of the effects of film in the 1930s)
- The availability of research funds (e.g., when the U.S. Surgeon General provided a multimillion-dollar research fund for the study of television violence on children in the 1960s)
- Adequate and appropriate research methods that often fit best with the study of certain research problems (e.g., Lazarsfeld's audience surveys of media effects)
- The dominant theoretical paradigm guiding this scholarly field

The Direction of Communication Research

Thirty-five years ago, it was believed that communication theory would unify all human knowledge. But this vision "began to fade almost before it was attempted."

> There is almost nothing to remind us that communication was once regarded as the master key, the common element in all the physical, natural, and social sciences, as well as the link between the sciences and the humanities. Communication has become a course among courses, a patchwork of courses scattered throughout a university curriculum, and taught often by people whose intellectual deficiencies are embarrassing [McCormack, 1986, p. 34].

Once the study of communication was classified as the academic property of just a single university department (or even two departments, such as mass media communication and interpersonal communication), its intellectual scope was limited. So the organizational structure of universities, especially in the United States in the 1950s and 1960s, posed barriers to fulfilling the integrative potential of communication theory. Communication became just another department within the university, and, to a large extent, just another social science. Its integrating vision got lost in its activities to become a discipline.

Today, some observers feel the opportunities presented by the new communication technologies might boost communication theory to a central position in understanding human behavior (Paisley, 1984), and thus to fulfilling somewhat its 1950s vision of unifying all knowledge. Compared to other social science disciplines, communication science is more concerned with technology. Most social sciences are neutral toward technology; their journals include few articles about the new media. Psychology and political science are not much concerned with communication technology. Sociology and anthropology may often be negative toward technology. These social scientists point to the unanticipated negative consequences of technology for society or at least for certain segments of society (Rogers, 1986). This function is indeed an important scholarly contribution, helping to counterbalance the unquestioningly positive perspective of many technologists. Sociologists like to point out that social structures often shape the way in which a technology is used; thus, this position might be called social determinism.

An antitechnology bias has not generally characterized communication scholars. Indeed, many communication scholars perceive computer science and electrical engineering as friendly intellectual cousins, at least they have in recent years. Communication research and information science are distinctive as social sciences in their relationship with electrical engineering (since the influence of Shannon in 1949) and, in recent years, with computer science. These intellectual influences from nonbehavioral science sources stem from the attention communication researchers and information scientists pay to communication technology.

Thus, communication scientists try to keep an open mind toward communication media, looking for empirical evidence about whether these media are associated with changes in society, whether the consequences are mainly positive or negative, and how social contexts influence the control, design, and use of such media. Certainly we should not assume that all new communication media are benign in their impacts. Nor should the new media be regarded as objects separate from their social context.

One of the reasons for academic interest in (and public support of) communication science over the past decades is its contribution in understanding the associations between individual, organizational, and social changes and new media. No one would claim that the study of communication effects is worthless; effects questions are fundamental to the study of human communication. On the other hand, most observers would argue that the heavy focus of U.S. communication scholars on investigating effects is overdone. Further, too much of the effects research has followed an oversimplified, one-way model of communication that ignores the context of communication, and falsely distorts its phenomenological nature by overlooking the inherent subjectivity of human interaction. Chapters 3 and 11 explore alternative research approaches that attempt to overcome these limitations and problems. Effects issues can be studied in ways that do not ignore context or subjectivity; however, communication research issues other than communication effects should be studied.

A major imperative for shifting the direction of communication research in the 1980s is the interactive nature of the new computer-based media. Linear models do not serve communication scholars well when the media are no longer one-way. Simple effects cannot be studied when the uses of the new media are complexly variable for each individual participant in a communication system. False dichotomies such as mass media versus interpersonal face-to-face communication channels, which have for too long divided the discipline, will likely fade in the face of the new forms of communication, which have certain similarities to, and differences from, both interpersonal and mass media communication (Reardon & Rogers, 1988; Rice, 1987b).

Paths Not Taken

The heavy emphasis of past communication scholars on investigating the effects of the newest medium has come at a cost in terms of what was *not* studied. Communication scholars typically ignored questions about the structure of the media industry. For example, the Payne Fund studies of the effects of movies on children (Charters, 1933) did not investigate the structure of the film industry. Nor did they address questions of film industry ownership, funding, control, and public oversight (Rowland, 1986). This lack of attention is strange as amelioration of the problems documented by the Payne Fund scholars certainly would call for changes in the industry (Wartella & Reeves, 1985). A parallel case to film emerged for the new communication medium of television in the 1950s and 1960s. The overwhelming focus was on the medium and its effects, while the organizational structures (i.e., the industry) providing the technology was left unstudied (Gitlin, 1983).

The telephone, along with such other two-way media as the telegraph and letters, has been almost totally ignored by communication scholars. "Western researchers seem to have invested more time and effort in examining the effects of the electronic mass media—radio and television—than the effects of the instrument on their desks which links them to other people and organizations" (Hudson, 1984, p. 5). This ignored medium has undergone a tremendous expansion worldwide; namely, from 41 million telephones in 1945 to 494 million in 1982, an increase of 1,200 percent. Nevertheless, the effects paradigm of communication scholars did not fit with the investigation of such nonlinear media as the telephone, telegraph, and letters, so these media were largely ignored by communication scholars, as shown by Ithiel de Sola Pool (1977, p. 2):

> Social scientists have neglected the telephone not only along with, but also relative to, other technologies. As a cause of social changes, transportation . . . has been much more studied than communication. And among communication media, TV, radio, movies, even the telegraph has been studied more than the telephone.

Pool (1977, p. 4) noted that the telephone's

> impacts are puzzling, evasive, and hard to pin down. . . . That conclusion does not imply that the phone has no impact or that there is nothing to study. On the contrary, it implies that the study of the telephone's social impact belongs to the important and subtle class of problems in the social sciences which demand a logic more complex than that of simple causality—a logic that allows for purposive behavior as an element in the analysis.

Past study of the telephone was shortchanged because the telephone was widely diffused among U.S. households before communication research took off around 1950. Obviously, the study of the telephone's diffusion and impact was made more difficult after the point at which almost all U.S. households had phones.

The function of the telephone has changed radically in recent years, focusing the creation of a new term, POTS (plain old telephone service), for the former functions of telephony, such as person-to-person voice contact at a distance. Now telephones also carry data and text from one computer to another, and provide voice messaging services. Moreover, there are likely to be many more changes in this current period of communication deregulation.

Computers and telephonic communication have only come together recently, in the 1980s. The full intellectual implications of this merger are not yet widely grasped by communication scholars, nor can they be fully understood for some years. But certainly the new communication media require increased attention to such topics as ownership and control and such new media as voice messaging systems and voice synthesization.

Communication Policy Analysis

In addition to social science research on the new media, which is the main concern of this book, the new media are also a favorite topic of communication policy analysts. Such analyses primarily deal with political, legal, economic, and philosophical dimensions of the new communication media. The types of research methods described in our present volume play only a minor role in forming communication policies. However, illustrations of some selected policy issues that have been the focus of policy analysis in recent years include:

Computer software copyright issues: Here a key issue is whether a computer program like the popular Lotus 1-2-3 can be "cloned" legally by another company's program that looks—and feels—the same on a computer screen, but whose written computer code may be entirely different.

Teletext advertising: Who is the owner of advertising messages broadcast by teletext? The Federal Communication Commission (FCC) has ruled that the local broadcaster owns the vertical blanking interval (in which the teletext message is conveyed) of a television signal. Hence the broadcaster should get incomes that derive from the sale of teletext advertising and may replace the teletext signal provided by a national network.

Copying off-the-air programs with a VCR: The U.S. courts ruled in the Sony Betamax decision of 1984 that anyone can legally record regular television broadcasts with a videocassette recorder, as long as the recordings are not for resale to others.

National and international standardization of products: The rate of diffusion of videotape recorders in the United States was slowed by the two competing brands (Betamax versus VHS). In contrast, the manufacturers of CD-ROM chips met at the High Sierra Casino and Hotel, Lake Tahoe, Nevada, in November 1984 to put forward an unofficial standard for CD-ROM manufacturers, specifying disc size, maximum amount of stored data, and error correction codes, and this has contributed to the rapid diffusion of this medium.

Deregulation of U.S. telephone service: With the divestiture of AT&T in 1984, we have embarked on a pattern of shifting major parts of the telephone industry from a protected monopoly to a type of protected competition. Although many of the arguments favoring deregulation hold that it offers economic benefits, there is little objective research on the issue. It is a challenge to regulators to understand the alternatives and consequences of telephone deregulation.

Much policy analysis has been conducted on each of these and many other issues, and it played a role in informing the policy decisions that were made in each case. Unfortunately, the present book cannot adequately cover the specialized methods used in policy analysis.

Expanding the Study of Media Technologies

Many older communication researchers were taught that communication technology should be the concern mainly of electrical engineers, physicists, and computer scientists, and that it had little significance for those trained as social scientists. This basic belief in the irrelevance of communication media continued through the 1960s, despite the popular writings of Marshall McLuhan, who, in such books as *Understanding Media: The Extensions of Man* (1964), claimed that such communication media as television were "extensions of man," broadening one's senses to enable individuals to reach farther out into their environment for information. Nevertheless, through the 1970s, most scholars in our field believed that media were a nonfactor in communication research.

Communication scholars tend to investigate each new communication medium, at least at first, using research approaches borrowed from the immediately previous technology. For example, the overwhelming majority of television studies focused primarily on the effects of message content (as had studies of the earlier mass media of film and radio). The emphasis of research on the violence and sex portrayed on television may have been in part an artifact inherited from previous film research. Ignored, at least initially, was the role of television in the creation of new social environments despite the writings of Marshall McLuhan, who claimed that television was a new sensory experience.

One of the first communication scholars to focus on the technologies of communication media was Edwin B. Parker, then a professor of communication at Stanford University, who had pioneered in research on computers and communication satellites. Parker, later to cofound a successful Silicon Valley satellite communication company, felt that technology variables should receive a greater focus in communication research. For example, he pointed out that field experiments on development communication in Third World nations seldom explained more than 10 percent or 20 percent of the variance in such dependent variables as knowledge about, and adoption of, health and agricultural innovations. In contrast, Parker and his associates might explain 70 percent to 80 percent of the variance in health adoption behaviors in studies of two-way satellite radio communication linking Eskimo and Indian villagers in Alaska with medical expertise. Instead of accepting communication technology as a given, Parker considered it as a *variable* that communication scholars could control, influence, and study. Parker (1973) concluded: "As new information technologies become available, a whole new program of research is required to learn technologies for their effective utilization." At the time, however, most communication scholars continued to doubt that the study of communication technology was a legitimate concern of communication scientists. This changed in 1973 with the founding of the Annenberg School of Communications at the University of Southern California. The new dean, Frederick Williams, citing Parker's arguments, positioned the school's curriculum and research concentrations on the new media.

The study of communication technology has today become widespread among communication scholars, with major research attention given to two issues: the adoption and use of these innovations, and the consequences associated with the use and control of new media. Adoption and use of the new media are studied more frequently than how technology influences social life. "There is an empirical vacuum of startling proportions on the social consequences of technology" (Fischer, 1985, p. 290).

One exception to the general lack of consequences research is the studies on the impact of VCRs. During the 1980s, videocassette recorders achieved a rapid rate of adoption by consumers in many nations: 50 percent of households in the United States, 30 percent in Japan, 40 percent in England, 70 percent in Saudi Arabia, and 90 percent in Kuwait. One analyst concluded that "The greatest potential threat to the total disintegration of national communication policy . . . is the videocassette recorder" (Ogan, 1985).

Most policymakers have not considered the VCR relevant to national communication policies, because the VCR is not a *mass* medium. Additionally, legal and illegal copying of videotapes, especially pornographic films and horror films, posed problems for national governments in controlling their television and film systems (Boyd & Straubhaar, 1985). Furthermore, the widespread diffusion of VCRs in certain countries—for example, Nigeria and Venezuela—created strong pressures for overcoming the government's original policy against color television broadcasting. Finally, nations with a high rate of adoption of VCRs are generally characterized in the 1980s by depressed film attendance (Ogan, 1985). A basic reason for the rapid adoption of VCRs in most nations is a desire for greater media diversity. When diversity is resricted to, say, a single government-operated television network that provides dull programs, the preconditions exist for a rapid rate of videocassette adoption. Here we see how one new medium impacts other mass media, in this case putting more control in the hands of the public.

Today, almost every school or department of communication at an American university employs at least one faculty member specializing in the new communication technologies, and offers undergraduate as well as graduate courses on this topic. Research on the new media is now a high priority for communication scholars. Communication majors today are increasingly required to enroll in computer-programming courses and to utilize computers in news writing and in television and film production, as well as in data-analysis. Our focus on new media seems to be appropriate for a social science that uniquely positions itself at the interface between human behavior and the information technologies that may change society.

Summary

In this chapter we discussed the considerable influence of each wave of new communication media (film, radio, television, and computers) on communication research. The dominant theoretical paradigm, the degree of public concern, the state of current research methodology, and other factors have affected the directions taken by past communication research. We think that the influence of changing communication media on the nature of communication research has not been sufficiently appreciated in past histories of the field. The topics studied by communication research obviously have an important influence on the research methods used to conduct such research. On the other hand, certain topics could not be studied adequately until the appropriate methods for such research became available. The study of communication effects did not proliferate (as measured by the number of studies conducted per year) until certain methodological developments such as measurement scales, sampling designs, survey methods, and computer data-analysis became available after World War II, and until the paradigm of a linear model of one-way communication (based on Claude Shannon's information theory) became popular among communication scholars in the 1950s.

Today, the paradigm of linear, one-way communication may be giving way to a more cybernetic paradigm (based on Norbert Wiener's theory) that better fits the interactivity of the new media. This basic change carries implications for using different theories and methods in future communication research.

CHAPTER 3

Choosing Among Alternative Research Designs

Conflicts Over Research Methods

The Chicago School of Sociology dominated the social sciences in the United States from 1915 to 1935. John Dewey, George Herbert Mead, and Robert Park, three of the important American "roots" of communications research, were then teaching at the University of Chicago. Much of the research that made the Chicago School famous was carried out in the urban slums that surrounded the university campus. For example, Park investigated the role of the foreign language press in the integration of new immigrants into U.S. society. Most of these investigations by the Chicago School were qualitative case studies of urban social problems: poverty, prostitution, racial prejudice, and crime. Robert Park called statistical methods "parlor tricks," but eventually the Chicago School began to incorporate quantitative research methods in their studies. Much conflict about the choice of methods arose at Chicago; even the graduate students at department picnics split into two softball teams on the basis of "the statisticians" versus "the qualitatives."

This conflict over research methods has continued to the present day, with a camp of dedicated quantitative scholars pitted against another camp of investigators using qualitative methods. We think this conflict is often taken to an extreme, as no research method is the most appropriate for *all* research problems. Each has different advantages, disadvantages, assumptions, biases, and degrees of usefulness.

The present chapter describes the main criteria for choosing among the wide variety of alternative methods for investigating the new media. Our focus is on research design, the plan for conducting a scientific study; on associated methods; and the tools for accomplishing the research design.

Conventional Approaches

In this section, we briefly describe eleven different approaches to the study of the new media that fall in the general category of conventional—that is, positivist and quantitative—research. They are arranged approximately along a quantitative-qualitative continuum, with the most quantitative approaches listed first.[1]

MATHEMATICAL MODELING

This type of research develops a closed set of equations in order to describe relationships among a set of phenomena. It may involve the manipulation of different values or ranges of values to detect consequences (direct, indirect, or lagged) of changing assumptions about the phenomena under study. Its strengths are in making assumptions explicit and stating descriptions in an unambiguous language. Its weaknesses are that it is highly dependent on initial assumptions, much prior knowledge about the phenomenon of study is necessary, and one is unable to analyze the influences of intervening variables. Chapter 5 describes one complex mathematical model for forecasting the diffusion of new media.

CONTROLLED EXPERIMENTS

Experiments manipulate one or a few known independent variables and determine the subsequent variation in one or several dependent variables. Mechanisms for decreasing error and increasing control include the random assignment of individual respondents to treatment conditions and the use of double-blind experiments (whereby experimenters are unaware of which subjects have been assigned to which conditions, and subjects are unaware of whether they are in a treatment or control group). Strengths include the minimization of error and prevention of possible alternative explanations for the research results, increased explanation of variance in phenomena because of controls, the ability to emphasize theory in choosing variables and conditions, and strong internal validity. As for weaknesses, because multiple variables are always operating, controlled experiments oversimplify a real-life situation in order to control certain of these variables. The trade-offs for the experimental approach, particularly in the study of human use of new media, include a lack of realism and unnaturally emphasized cues from the media of study and from other individuals in the experiment. Often the research situation has no history and no future, and involves a small number of participants who are often neither randomly selected nor randomly assigned to conditions.

QUASI-EXPERIMENTS

The partially controlled "field" experiment occurs in natural settings with naturally occurring differences in the presence and timing of conditions. They usually involve control over the timing of measurement and the choice of respondents, but do not allow the researcher to assign subjects to different experimental conditions. Because field experiments are natural phenomena and typically occur over time, they can effectively portray some of the context, history, and social realities that influence the use and interpretation of new media. Therefore, external validity of field experiments is stronger than in controlled experiments. Weaknesses include finding appropriate research sites, maintaining the intended design or process in light of real changes and constraints in the site, and guaranteeing that these changes are not the primary influence on the experimental results. Field trials of new media systems typically risk the bias of studying the behavior of unusually innovative respondents.

SURVEYS

This type of research employs questionnaires, more or less structured, that allow researchers to gather data by mail, telephone, online, or face-to-face interviews, usually from a large sample of respondents. Surveys are typically cross-sectional—that is, they gather data at only one time period. A useful variant type of survey is "group feedback analysis," which asks members of a group to respond to a survey, and then provides the results as feedback to the group so that it may interpret them and elaborate on their meaning and on the assumptions behind the questions and responses. Among the strengths of surveys is that they can measure many variables, thus allowing statistical analysis of multiple and complex relationships. They can be used iteratively to refine hypotheses and questions. Recent approaches emphasize asking just a few questions over numerous time periods to many individuals randomly selected each time.

Among the weaknesses is that surveys do not reveal the different underlying motivations or interpretations that lead to similar responses on a questionnaire—that is, surveys are not effective in answering "why" questions. Also, they emphasize analyses of an aggregated set of individuals. The goal is often the explanation of shared variance at a point in time instead of the process of a phenomenon. They assume a static system in equilibrium, and they encourage the interpretation of a statistical association between two variables as evidence of a causal relationship from one variable to another.

LONGITUDINAL STUDIES

Longitudinal studies encompass data on units of analysis either at discrete time periods or continuously over a period of time. The units may be the same sample of respondents (a panel study), different samples (a pooled cross-sectional time-series), a single variable (a time-series), or different sets of people moving through the same stages in a process (a cohort study). Longitudinal studies can be contextual—that is, concerned with the description of a phenomenon in its internal and external contexts over time. The strength of longitudinal studies is the explicit consideration of the belief that phenomenon exist and are revealed over time. They allow insight into processes that may take time to develop, and identify short-run and long-run usage patterns of a new medium, diffusion trends, and changes in social realities. The weakness is that they are costly and time-consuming. A rigid design may not be able to adjust to changing contexts and conditions (such as the development of new uses or forms of the medium during the study).

FIELD STUDIES

Research in field study designs involves observations and measurement of naturally occurring phenomena for which there are no known natural or experimental controls. Field studies can consist of a combination of conventional methods (case studies, questionnaire surveys, and archival data) conducted under naturalistic conditions over time. Among the strengths are that the dependent variable(s) are systematically measured in the context of a natural setting. Field studies can provide insight into phenomena as they ordinarily occur. As for weaknesses, field studies do not allow the researcher to isolate specific processes and influences among a range of alternate explanations. No control over characteristics of respondents or of conditions is possible. Field studies are often weak in internal validity.

Archival and Secondary Research

This approach involves the collection and analysis of historical data, or the re-analysis of data collected by prior researchers. In both cases the data may have been collected for other purposes. For example, a historical trail of legal documents might be inspected to understand how corporate and government interests prevented the development of common standards in videotext. Among the strengths are possibly lower cost and understanding of historical processes. Other strengths include the ability to identify past trends as a baseline for comparison with current processes. Also, secondary research guarantees that the researcher is not intervening in the topic of study through the data-gathering process (although this may have occurred when the data were first collected). As for weaknesses, the data may not be in a form suited for the researcher's goals. There may be biases in ways the data were originally sampled, collected, and preserved. The way indices are calculated to compare trends may have changed over time, and the variables measured may not reflect the secondary researcher's exact concerns.

Futures Research and Forecasting

Futures research attempts to define plausible directions that a phenonenon of interest will take based on techniques such as scenarios, Delphi surveys, market trend analysis, and the content analysis of popular media (Chapter 5).

A strength of futures research is that it forces a consideration of possible consequences of current policies and uncovers assumptions behind predictions. The weakness, however, is that it is unable to specify all relevant factors. It tends to overestimate early aspects of change, while underestimating long-run consequences. It can generate political conflict or co-optations and can misconstrue relationships among variables related to predictions.

CONTENT ANALYSIS

Content analysis is the systematic and reliable coding of communication content into a theoretically meaningful set of mutually exclusive and exhaustive categories. The message content can come from television programs (such as verbal content, physical relationships, visual and aural techniques, or scene settings), transcribed radio speeches, and written texts (such as newspaper stories or an ongoing dialogue through electronic mail). The content can be analyzed qualitatively (to develop an understanding of the use and form of various content) or quantitatively (as frequencies or percentages of one category compared to another, or to determine the reliability of coding). Computer-monitored data from a computer bulletin board system can be automatically content analyzed to identify common topics of public discourse (Chapter 6).

Strengths are that content analyses can be used to describe trends in content over time. It provides a theoretical connection between the intentions of individuals and organizations producing media content and possible social consequences related to audience use of that content. It can test theories about the meaning of messages. Weaknesses are that content is often stripped of both its context and of the development of meaning occurring through relationships of the communication participants. Transcribing and coding messages is usually lengthy and costly. Content analysis may encourage the assumption that message content has specific effects.

CASE STUDIES

A case study involves the observation, description, or reconstruction of a phenomenon of interest. In a conventional case study, the researcher does not intervene in the phenomenon of study. Other forms of the case study, such as those involving participant observation, require the researcher to become part of the social context to understand it more adequately (Chapter 7). For example, a researcher might become a user of an organization's new electronic mail system to better describe the ways in which users developed forms of conversational etiquette that were different from those in their face-to-face communication. As a strength, a case study can describe complex relationships, personal interpretations, and historical narratives of the phenomenon. Weaknesses are that case studies are typically limited to a single setting or set of individuals, often rely on the reconstruction of past events, and are susceptible to multiple interpretations. Also, researchers may intervene in the phenomenon of interest, perhaps by influencing the actions and interpretations of the respondents.

FOCUS GROUPS

The general approach of focus groups is to bring from two to ten people together to discuss their reactions to a limited, but not explicitly bounded, set of concepts, products, problems, or design considerations. An experienced focus group moderator leads the discussion to develop a range of emotional and cognitive responses and to pursue a set of desired topics. As for strengths, an experienced analyst can "read" transcripts or recordings from focus groups to generate new concepts or understandings, such as what a new office technology means to organizational members and how it might affect their existing work relationships. Focus groups can "provide the opportunity to observe informants conducting their own discursive tests, negotiating meaning, and confirming or disconfirming appropriate ways of speaking" (Hiemstra, 1983, p. 807). Weaknesses are that focus groups are susceptible to domination by a particular respondent or to the biases of the moderator. Focus group participants are often atypical of the intended population of study. The results of focus group discussions are usually qualitative and hence not suitable for statistical analysis.

Assumptions and Criticisms of
Conventional Positivist Approaches[2]

A French sociologist of the mid-nineteenth century, Auguste Comte, first talked of research "positivism" because he was positive scientific methods could be usefully applied to the study of human behavior in order to identify and help solve social problems. Also, Comte felt that social theory should be based on "positive" (real) empirical facts. This original meaning of positivism meant that scientific methods were mainly borrowed from the biological and physical sciences, which were much older than the emerging social sciences. The basic design for the laboratory experiment was borrowed from physics and chemistry. Most of the research designs and methods borrowed from the physical sciences were quantitative. So positivism over the years took on the implication of a belief in the application of quantitative scientific methods.

Several assumptions underlie the positivist approach:

- The scientific method is appropriate for most topics of inquiry.
- The goal of inquiry is to identify causal relationships.
- The basis for analysis can be experienced by the human senses; mental speculation or notions of nonmaterial forces are not acceptable evidence.
- The process of science is value free.
- The basic foundation of science is mathematics and logic.
- The focus of study is a real, objective world.
- The basis for belief in, and credibility of, research results is the ability to (1) replicate them in similar circumstances, and (2) define how the results will vary in different circumstances. This criterion of replicability requires that data and results be freely shared and implies that scientific knowledge is cumulative.

The positivist paradigm has been criticized as having at least four major flaws (Bonoma, 1985; Kersten, 1986; Mumford et al., 1985). First, at the early stages of any discipline or theory, narrow, rigorous, and predefined research methods are inappropriate because they hinder the possibility of discovering new aspects that are not measurable or analyzable using prior methods. Multiple, process-oriented research methods should be used to investigate novel conditions.

Second, conventional designs, data-collection, and analytical tools are not adequate on "their own in areas involving human activity" (Mumford et al., 1985). Past scientific procedures often treat humans as manipulable objects stripped of their social contexts, their historical processes, the subjective interpretations and meanings that they attribute to actions or develop within their social sphere, and their rights to participate in the process of discovering knowledge about their situation. "Effects" are assumed to exist and to be "caused" in a unidirectional fashion by certain independent variables rather than social realities being mutually created and interpreted in changing ways by social participants and interactions between different levels of reality. The conventional positivist approach has been criticized for assuming that social phenomena and structures are concrete facts that exist prior to human activity rather than being socially constructed through communication, symbols, and behaviors.

Critics of the conventional approach to communication research argue that the particular contexts of human behavior are not replicable, that values inhere not only in researchers but also in scientific methods and theories, and that many important concepts—such as meaning—cannot be precisely measured. Insofar as events are interdependent and contextual, human behavior should be understood as rule-following rather than as causally determined. Relationships are probabilistic, and meaningfulness is the essential criterion for understanding human behavior. Because concerns about the new media involve social, economic, and political issues rather than just technical ones, the positivist research approach cannot alone provide adequate theoretical guidance, methodological relevance, or practical benefits.

Third, the conventional research approach cannot easily generate explicit alternatives to its assumptions and perspectives. It focuses on identifying and falsifying alternate explanations *within* its framework (Chapter 4). Instead, scientific paradigms should be seen as "contending social realities, different interpretive realities, with their own internally defensible criteria" (Kersten, 1986). Researchers in practice do not follow completely the principles of positivism; the process of research is fundamentally incremental, intuitive, and unpredictable. Science is a search for understanding, so procedures for understanding may come in many forms.

Fourth, the conventional research approach has many other practical and policy limitations. For example, the operationalization of most variables is an indirect measure of the phenomenon (concept) under study. Most studies explain only a small amount of variance. Few research reports are comparable; thus the assumption of replicability and cumulation in science is not upheld in practice. Multivariate research, necessary to specific complex relationships, simultaneously makes results impractical or ambiguous for translation into practice. Finally, and perhaps most disturbing to some researchers and theorists, those phenomena not susceptible to, or deemed appropriate by, conventional social science methods, are not studied.

Alternatives to Conventional Research Methods and Designs

SOURCES AND RATIONALES

Out of the contemporary debate about positivism has come alternative theories and paradigms for understanding human communication. These alternatives are broadly called the interpretive and critical approaches. It is perhaps better to describe this movement as a re-emergence of several qualitative and philosophical strands that have developed over the centuries alongside the more conventional positivist approach in social science.

One of the sources of the interpretive paradigm is Max Weber, a German sociologist who wrote his most famous books around the turn of the century. He argued that the task of the social scientist was not to describe events objectively through an observer's perspective, but to determine the subjective meanings of events to the participants in such actions. Human behavior, said Weber, can be understood only through the subjective meanings of the causes and consequences of social action. *Verstehen* is the empathic understanding by the scientific observer of an individual's actions. To gain such understanding, a social scientist must set aside rules of thinking that are taken for granted and instead attempt to enter into the respondent's thinking. Only in this way can propositions about human behavior account for the meaning of communication messages.

Two characteristics of interpretive research usually follow from its central belief in the importance of subjective meanings. First, it is primarily inductive, moving in focus from the empirical level up to the theoretical level. Starting with data (usually qualitative data) does not mean that theory is absent, but, instead, that theory plays a different role than in the positivist approach, where theoretical implications are tested by hypotheses about relationships among concepts that have been operationalized at the empirical level. Theory defines the objectives of interpretive research interest and guides the formation of propositions from data about the subjective meanings of the actors in a social context. Second, interpretive investigators emphasize the holistic setting in which some action or event takes place. This context is not just the environment surrounding the action or event, but the meaning of this context to the individuals involved.

Although the interpretive approach in general rejects conventional social science methods, there is no unified methodology associated with the schools of the interpretive or critical approach. However, the interpretive approaches have at least the following principles in common. First, individuals create their own realities, and they must evaluate and interpret this system of constraints on their behavior—that is, interpretations are individually subjective as well as constructed in interaction with other individuals through communication processes. Because reality is jointly created, and the more dominant forces play a larger role in this creation, contradictions always exist in the social world. Further, social reality is always distorted in some fashion, such as through paradigms and ideologies, often to legitimate, hide, or re-interpret existing social relations.

Second, elements of this reality are not isolatable or separable; both individual action and structural conditions mutually influence each other. Below the surface realities and material conditions exist deeper meanings and social structures, such as assumptions about the beneficial role of new communication media, or the advantages of a free-market economy in allocating resources for the development of those new media.

Third, approaches differ to the extent to which the research activities are inherently critical. Conventional approaches are seen as unconsciously supporting the status quo. Putnam (1983) distinguishes between the naturalist and the critical branches of the interpretive approach. The former attempts to understand how society is regulated and stabilized (through the negotiation and creation of meaning). The critical approach, however, is consciously dedicated to identifying, evaluating, and removing social inequity, domination, and distortions.

As with the conventional methods, the interpretative approach has weaknesses, too. Some of these include difficulties in managing and summarizing the large amounts of qualitative data such as field notes and transcripts, an avowed subjectivity in collecting and integrating materials, providing a public record of the basis of conclusions, and identifying and presenting multiple relations. Further, there is often a reluctance to use computer-based tools because they appear to represent the technocratic and depersonalized aspects of the positivist tradition, even though they are fundamentally distinct from the interpretative process itself (Das, 1983).

There is no single method that solves these criticisms, but we can say that the research method that best contributes to a deep understanding of these principles is the most appropriate. Four basic methodological processes underlie the interpretivist paradigm:

1. Consciously critique the theoretical and methodological assumptions through an emphasis on revealing contradictions, testing assumptions about the deep structure, and questioning the forms of power that are taken for granted. For example, most designers and marketers of videotext incorrectly relied on conventional assumptions about information as a commodity for which mass audiences in the United States are interested in searching and paying. These assumptions ignored ritualistic, symbolic, and entertainment purposes of media use (Dozier and Rice, 1984).

2. Describe the phenomenon of interest in ways that reflect the meanings of, and thus are recognizable by, those participating in the situation. Then redescribe it in ways that reveal the complexity of historic, social, and economic contexts and relations involved. Allow description, categories, methods, and explanation to constantly interact in order to allow the complexities of the situation to emerge from ongoing attempts at understanding. For example, Hiemstra (1983) identified cultural categories of meanings associated with office automation, then redescribed them in terms of their linkages, and next redescribed those in terms of guiding metaphors.

3. Make explicit links between macro- and micro-analyses. For example, Schiller (1982) and Mosco (1982) use UNESCO documents, annual corporate reports, and economic data on trade flows to describe how multinational corporations' use of telecommunication networks reflect and perpetuate global stratification into core, semi-peripheral, and peripheral regions.

4. Direct the research toward developing knowledge that can contribute to positive social change.

The next sections summarize three particular directions in the alternative paradigm to positivism, concentrating on their applicability in the study of new media.

INTERPRETIVE APPROACH

The *interpretive approach* to communication research emphasizes the subjective meanings of communication messages by the actors in a system (Geertz, 1973). How such individuals interpret messages is often best studied by methods that are qualitative and less-struc-

tured. Whereas conventional theories tend to assume that members
of systems (such as organizations) share common goals and will cooperate to achieve them if conditions are supportive, the interpretive
approach includes:

- Considering roles as sets of rights and duties, or social contracts,
  that govern social behavior in ways that fit the sources and content of current beliefs.
- Analyzing decision making as the content, process, and location
  of examining a problem and creating meaning, based on a mix-
  ture of evidence, intuition, analysis, negotiation, and value
  judgments.
- Understanding the transactions involved in acquiring, exchanging, and distributing information, and the collective or hierarchical sources (such as policies, rituals, and ceremonies) of
  communication systems.
- Identifying how communication mediates individuals' intentions
  and behaviors, either through defensible, valid reasons or by
  vested interests and conventions (Habermas, 1984).

Interpretive research has been used especially to understand how
interactions among individuals, groups, and cultures in organizations
influence the interpretation and success of office automation systems
(Hirschheim, 1985).

A particularly relevant example of applying the interpretive approach to the study of new media is Streeter's (1987) discourse analysis
of policy debates and the evolution of cable television. By analyzing the language and metaphors used by the various proponents of
cable television—a language of revolutionary and liberating technology—Streeter showed that the common discourse fostered an alliance among groups (such as the cable industry, professional groups,
and liberal organizations) that would ordinarily have been opposed
because of the nature of their special interests. In the end, this alliance
obscured the underlying conflicts and subverted the goals of the
language: "the discourse helped shape an institution that it failed to
describe" (p. 174). The author notes that the 1984 Cable Act finalized
and legitimized the commercial, corporate form of cable provision.

CONTEXTUALISM

Contextualism argues that individuals, organizations, events, or
structures should not be isolated from the ongoing interdependencies

that both constrain and generate change in human behavior. Instead, communication research should describe the context, content, and process of change as part of an ongoing process, background, or structure. Contextualism represents a protest against the positivistic research approach of investigating human behavior as a kind of individualistic "psychology," assuming that the setting in which the behavior or study takes place is unimportant in understanding behavior. Guidelines for contextual research include conducting comparative case studies of the new media in different settings, studying multiple incidents in the same setting but at different points in time, and investigating different phases of the same communication system.

For example, a contextual analysis of a new electronic messaging system would consider system design, organizational and individual adoption processes, ongoing implementation, re-invention of the new medium, conflicts over ownership and applications, and short-term and long-term implications. Contextual research also balances description and analysis. It specifies the choice of the beginning and the end of the time interval of study, thus focusing a study on the historical background of the behavior of study. It investigates multiple interpretations from multiple data-sources and uses different levels of analysis.

Much of the failure of the early promises for communication technology to assist in Third World Development can be attributed to the lack of contextualization of much research based on experiences in developed countries. Third World countries experience considerably different contexts that affect why communication technologies are adopted, how they are interpreted, and to what purposes they are used. External contexts include their position on the periphery of the transnational economy, unequal trade relationships, and dependency on economic and material aid. Internal contexts include cultural differences (such as religion, race, family structures), economic differences (distribution of income, access to media), and political differences (the influence of a single political party, military and bureaucratic pressures). Mody (1985) shows how these factors contribute to different needs, uses, and experiences of communication technologies in Third World contexts.

ACTION RESEARCH

Action research is a type of investigation combining practice and theory that is designed to both cooperate with as well as support less-enfranchised actors and groups in a system of study. Researchers following the action research paradigm explicitly question the acceptance of the status quo, patterns of control, normative choices about technology, and operating constraints on action and choices. Most funding for research on computer-based information systems is strongly influenced by positivist researchers, technical designers, and organizational managers. Action research seeks to balance this possible bias.

Action research attempts to combine practice and theory by:

- Providing feedback to all relevant actors in the system of study.
- Providing continuous feedback to the respondents of the study.
- Participation by the researcher in the process of change.
- Developing alternate actions for the participants in the system.
- Considering actors as participants in, rather than objects of, the research process.
- Enabling researchers, practitioners, and respondents to gain from the research process.
- Attempting to balance the needs of multiple sets of actors with needs of the researcher (e.g., access to initial sources of data compared to concerns about confidentiality, and later publication of the research results to academic audiences compared to survey feedback to the users).

Action research has been used in the context of designing and implementing large-scale information systems by organizations and governments that support participative management and quality of work-life issues.

Criteria for Choosing Among Designs and Methods

Bonoma (1985) suggests three basic criteria that a researcher may use to evaluate the appropriateness of a proposed project's design orientation.

1. Is the purpose of the research that of exploration, description, or explanation? *Exploration* is a type of research that provides a beginning familiarity with a research topic, and it is necessary in order to develop theories about a phenomenon of interest. *Description* is a type of research that provides the context for both adjusting and testing a theory. *Explanation* is a type of

research that tests the extent to which a theory adequately represents the phenomenon being studied. More qualitative methods that provide deeper understanding, greater generalizability, higher external validity, and more adaptability to ongoing results may be more useful at the theory-building stages of research (exploration and description), while more quantitative methods may be more useful for theory-testing (explanation).

2. Can the phenomenon of interest usefully be studied independent from its context? If not, then research methods that emphasize content, interpretation, and meaning are more appropriate.

3. Are the phenomena under study amenable to quantification? If quantifiable, what is the best way to characterize the topic of study? Perhaps verbalization and narration are the more appropriate ways to describe, analyze, or explain the phenomenon.

Once these basic questions have been answered, the researcher then must evaluate a wide range of choices about variables, validity, cost, and research ethics. Table 3–1 lists some of the more specific criteria that should be considered in choosing research methods.

A Triangulation Example in the Study of Word Processing

It is often advantageous when doing research to use a variety of methods and collect multiple kinds of data. This process, called triangulation, comes originally from navigation, where multiple reference points are used to locate an exact position. Multiple measurements can converge to provide a more accurate operationalization of a concept than can any of the single measures. The logic for triangulation is that the weaknesses of any single method, qualitative or quantitative, are balanced by the strengths of the other methods. In the following example, Johnson and Rice (1987) used a variety of data-sources, research designs, and analytical methods to study the adoption of word processing by different organizations.

First, telephone interviews were conducted with representatives of 200 organizations to learn the extent to which word processing was used, the characteristics of each organization, and a brief description of the implementation process that had occurred in each organization. Then, sixty of the 200 organizations, stratified by industry and geo-

Table 3–1.   Some Conventional Criteria for Selecting Research Methods

1. Number of cases: Is a single case enough for some diversity, or is a large number needed to ensure a wide range of relations?
2. Access to respondents: To what extent is permission or a consent form required from respondents and institutions?
3. Level of measurement for each variable: Are measurements to be nominal (unordered categories), ordinal (an ordering of categories along a single dimension), interval (an ordering along a single dimension at equal intervals but with no true zero), or ratio (an ordering along a single dimension on an absolute scale that has a true zero point)?
4. Unit of analysis, the object of measurement: Is the unit of study to be individual persons, messages, events; groups, institutions, systems; or relationships among individuals, groups, organizations, nations?
5. Levels of analysis, the location of the phenomenon of study: Is the location to be individuals, dyads, small groups, communities, organizations, countries, or societies?
6. Variables: Do they provide sufficient variance, explanatory power, reliability, and validity? What is the necessary range of values? How many variables are necessary to conceptualize and measure? Are the values likely to vary? A *variable* is a qualitative or quantitative entity that can take on different values. A *dependent* variable is the main variable that a researcher wishes to understand or explain in a study. A researcher will use a particular theory to explain why variation in an *independent* variable is associated with some of the variation in the dependent variable. An *intervening* variable affects the relationship between an independent variable and dependent variable (it may make the relationship seem stronger or weaker than it really is).
7. Control: Does the research setting avoid unmeasurable or confounding conditions that are sources of error and alternative explanations? Are respondents assigned randomly to experimental conditions and measurements? Can the researcher adapt a project to respond to problems in design, respondents' concerns, or new insights?
8. Artifacts: Can the researcher identify or avoid threats to the validity or reliability of a research project because of confounding or alternative sources of variation?
9. Setting: How realistic or natural is the research context; are there possible biasing influences on respondents?
10. External validity: How generalizable are the findings to other respondents, settings, or time periods?
11. Internal validity: To what extent is the research measuring and testing what it claims to be?
12. Reliability: How replicable is the research process, measures, and results?
13. Design options: Can the researcher develop different sequences and controls for settings, conditions, and respondents?
14. Sampling design: What is required: a census (100 percent sample), a nonprobability sample (convenience or quota), a random sample (simple, systematic, stratified), or a hybrid sample (stratified cluster)?
15. Effectiveness: What is the utility and importance of the results compared to cost

(continued)

Table 3-1. *(Continued)*

and variables used, with respect both to the possible information available from the study and the possible information about the phenomenon from all kinds of methods?

16. Time frame: How appropriate is the design and the methods for studying the past, present, or future, or for studying processes versus a set of relations at a single point in time?

17. Cost: What are the full financial and social costs of the initial development of the research project; per respondent; during the life of the project; to the researcher, participants, and institutions?

18. Source of funding: How possible is it to gain support from a volunteer, personal, university, organization, nonprofit granting agency, or consulting funds; what contraints or advantages do each of these have?

19. Decision rule for testing hypotheses: What are the explicit bases determining whether a hypothesis received support or was rejected: none, judgment, statistical?

20. Ethics: Are respondents' rights, researchers' assumptions, and the larger social purposes of research considered?

SOURCE: Adapted from Jenkins (1985). See also Chapter 4 for a detailed discussion of some of these criteria.

graphical location in the United States, were selected for site visits. At each organization, the researchers conducted personal interviews with key managers, word-processing operators, and authors of word-processed documents and reviewed archival documents about the organization's implementation process for word processing. Finally, a questionnaire survey was administered to the population of word-processing managers and operators in each organization, and to a convenience sample of document authors.

Data were therefore collected at a variety of levels of analysis (organizational, departmental, job type, and individual) by a variety of methods (telephone and questionnaire survey, personal interviews, and archival materials) to make possible a variety of analyses (case studies, industry-level descriptions, and multivariate tests of hypotheses).

The telephone survey was an inexpensive way to gather a large amount of detailed data about an industry-level phenomenon. It also provided organizational-level data that could be merged with the individual-data collected later in the site interviews. The site visits allowed the researchers to develop a qualitative understanding of the particular contexts of each organization and its work units. Personal interviews revealed individual-level views of the political processes associated with the implementation of word processing and the processes of interaction that led to shared interpretations of work design and office technology. The questionnaire survey allowed the collection of standardized scales concerning group communication as well as individual demographic and attitudinal data on particular uses of word processing. Conducting these questionnaire surveys among three different job categories allowed an analysis of differences in various perceptions, such as perceptions of supervisory leadership. The qualitative data were used to develop a framework for identifying levels of innovative uses of word processing and to provide narrations of extreme cases; the questionnaire data were used to model the interactions among many variables and to summarize average trends across cases.

Although each of these data-collection or analytical approaches have certain known as well as unknown biases, this triangulation research design helped to identify and counterbalance such biases. More information on triangulation may be found in Webb et al. (1966); Jick (1979); Faules (1982); and Albrecht and Ropp (1982).

Summary

Every research design, method, and paradigm has strengths and weaknesses. No one alternative can produce perfect research; indeed, there is no such thing as perfect research. The scholar who only conducts experiments, or surveys, or participant observation, or historical analysis is limited. Important advances in science have usually come from a combination of loose and strict thinking and methods (Bateson, 1972). Thus, scholars have recently emphasized the need for triangulation.

One main theme in this chapter has been that no single research design or method is the *most* appropriate choice for studying any particular research problem, for there is a wide range of criteria that may be used in choosing which approach to use. Another main theme is that because research on the new media is at an early stage in its development, scholars studying it probably need to consider use of multiple methods, including more qualitative and triangulation methods of data-gathering and analysis, and the interpretive approaches to research. To date, however, most research on the new media has used only quantitative research methods and has been cast in a positivistic approach.

Notes

1. Portions of this section are adapted from Jenkins (1985). The reader is urged to consult some of the many excellent research methods books for further details about conventional research designs and methods, such as Anderson, 1987; Babbie, 1983; Kerlinger, 1973; Stempel and Westley, 1981; and Wimmer and Dominick, 1987.

2. This and the following sections are based on extensive discussions by Anderson, 1987; Bantz, 1983; Burrell & Morgan, 1979; Kersten, 1986, 1987; McGrath, 1982; Morgan, 1983; Mumford et al., 1985; Putnam, 1983; and Putnam and Pacanowsky, 1983. The reader is encouraged to read these and related sources (such as Smith, 1988) for a more detailed treatment of the interpretive and critical paradigms.

PART II

Problems and Solutions for Research

CHAPTER 4

Validity, Reliability, and Sampling

Requirements of Research Designs

Research design is a blueprint or plan for conducting a study. It identifies the sequence of measurements, sample selection, variables to be related to other variables, and the data-analysis methods to be used. Operationalizing a research design usually involves providing explicit descriptions of the language, timing, conditions, and respondents used in a study. Effective research designs according to conventional research criteria include: (1) reflecting natural settings and realistic influences, (2) showing clear relationships among causes and effects, (3) controlling extraneous variables, (4) excluding alternate explanations for the results, (5) exhibiting strong validity, and (6) demonstrating reliability of the research procedures and results. Achieving these conditions of effective research design is particularly difficult in the study of the new media.

We begin this chapter by briefly summarizing one research team's experiences in attempting to achieve these conditions in their study of a new medium. We then define important elements of research design; note key issues pertaining to validity, reliability, and sampling; and end by discussing appropriate designs and analysis methods to study processes associated with new media over time.

A Case Study of Teletext Research

Professors Martin Elton and John Carey of the Alternate Media Center of New York University evaluated a pilot teletext system through laboratory and field research in natural settings (Elton & Carey, 1984). Their experiences are summarized here as an introduction to the special problems of validity and reliability in the study of new media. They were forced to change their original research design by the context and settings in which the teletext system was used. But they were able to conduct significant and rigorous research because they understood ways in which satisfactory validity, reliability, and sampling could be achieved in the research project.

Originally, their research design incorporated two stages. The first stage was centered around a teletext information service with a small set of specialized information. Two pilot field trials provided the service. The first involved forty user homes, and a control group of another forty homes that did not have access to the service. Data would be gathered by personal interviews, diaries kept by the users, and computer-monitored records of teletext use. The second field trial involved ten public places, with data collected by observing patterns of users' movement around the teletext terminals and the behavior of nearby people. Here the "treatment"—the set of specialized information delivered by teletext—was similar. The control homes were intended to strengthen the internal validity of conclusions about changes over time in the user homes. The public sites were intended to increase external validity of the findings about teletext used in different settings. The first phase also involved laboratory studies of users' responses to various interface designs of the teletext system. This controlled setting allowed the researchers to control for and measure sources of differences in users' responses to teletext.

The second phase was to have been an expanded field trial, involving a general teletext information service with an expanded set of information, to test the effects of diverse programs. The respondents were to include a purposive sample of 300 households that used the teletext system and a control group of households that did not use the system. This larger sample would allow more complex multivariate analyses and reduce "type II" error—not finding significant results when they exist—caused by the small sample size of the first phase.

However, the shift to a natural setting (from stage one to stage two) created a variety of obstacles to validity, reliability, and sampling planned in the original research design. Multiple stakeholders had varying interests in the research project, including the FCC, the National Telecommunications and Information Administration, the Corporation for Public Broadcasting (CPB), hardware and software vendors, cable and commercial television operators, and information providers. These stakeholders often had opposing suggestions for which research questions should receive the most emphasis. For example, vendors wished to obtain evidence for technical feasibility of teletext, while CPB wished to obtain evidence as to how users could obtain nonprofit information. The research team also found it was difficult to acquire the skills to manage a politically visible public service.

The scarcity of prototype teletext technology (special transmission equipment and television decoders) led to technical difficulties and delays in obtaining the needed teletext equipment. Further, reception of the teletext signal by the sample homes was generally poor because of unexpected interference in the teletext broadcast area. The consequence was that different users received signals with different levels of quality, a threat to internal validity. Some users had access to the system for shorter periods of time, which also affected the sample. Because this nonprofit pilot service was clearly less satisfactory than an ongoing service with tested equipment and signal, the external validity of the results was threatened.

Also, since there were other sources of teletext service in the city, it was difficult to select and maintain a control group that would not be exposed to the teletext broadcasting treatment in the field experiment, which threatened internal validity and made sampling more difficult.

As a result of these problems, the forty-household control group had to be abandoned to identify a sufficient number of homes with good teletext reception. This decision, of course, made it impossible to defend against the criticism that responses from the users were *not* due to changes in homes or society in general instead of being due solely to the use of teletext. Even then, about 25 percent of the resulting sample of households continued to have inadequate teletext reception. Producing the teletext frame information was more costly and time-consuming than expected, and funding became more difficult as other pilot teletext systems were developed. Therefore, Phase II was canceled in favor of an extended Phase I.

Elton and Carey (1984) were, in the end, able to draw conclusions about response time, graphics, content, and placement of the teletext services. But their most important research results were lessons learned about the difficulties in following a conventional research design in evaluating a new medium in a realistic setting. They recommended that researchers of similar new media:

• Use Nielsen-like meters on the teletext terminal to collect programming, use, and error date (see Chapter 6).

- Use multiple measures of each concept (Chapter 3).
- Plan each research phase in a project to stand alone so that it will have some value if it is necessary to alter or drop other phases.
- Use early results as formative evaluation information for implementing and analyzing subsequent research conditions (Chapter 8).
- Explicitly identify qualifications about research results from a field experiment of a new medium.
- Identify the salient research questions early in the development of this new medium. (The Elton-Carey study was one of the first investigations of teletext in the United States.)

Elton and Carey (1984) attempted to follow the guidelines of rigorous conventional research methods, but the realities of a new medium made this impossible. By being flexible and aware of alternatives to their initial research design, the researchers were able to control for, or at least identify, possible threats to the reliability and validity of their study.

Elements of Research Design

VALIDITY

Validity is the degree to which a measure or a research design accurately operationalizes the concept it is intended to measure. Validity is analogous to the accuracy with which a dart thrower hits the bull's-eye.

Internal validity is the extent to which a measure or research design operationalizes what it purports to study in a way that prevents alternate explanations for the results (Campbell & Stanley, 1963; Cook & Campbell, 1979). These alternate explanations are often referred to as "rival hypotheses" or "artifacts." If plausible, they must be avoided or rejected before the intended hypothesis can be considered as a primary explanation for the phenomenon of interest. Table 4–1 lists common possible alternate explanations, with examples from the new media.

External validity is the extent to which a research study's results are generalizable, meaningful, useful, and applicable to situations and samples other than those studied. They should also be applicable to the specific population of interest that motivated the research (such as

Table 4–1. Common Alternate Explanations That Threaten the Internal Validity of a Research Study, Including Examples with New Media

1. History: Features of a new medium undergo technical changes during the course of the research project.
2. Maturation: Users gain increased experience with the new medium over time.
3. Testing: Interviews with potential users about their expectations concerning a new medium may alter these expectations before users try the new medium.
4. Instrumentation: Self-report data have different kinds of biases or errors than computer-monitored data.
5. Regression toward the mean: Results from a pilot system may be misleading insofar as the long-term trend is less pronounced.
6. Mortality: Respondents discontinue their use of a new medium before a pilot study is complete.
7. Selection: Individuals who volunteer to be part of an experimental evaluation of a new medium are atypical of those for whom the new medium is being designed.
8. Demand characteristics: Respondents may want to appear to researchers to be more innovative about a new technology than they in fact are.
9. Experimenter bias: Trainers may be too technical in explaining the use of a new medium or they hold assumptions about potential users that influence how the users interpret the instructions.
10. Response bias: Respondents may feel that a proper response to a question about their use of computers is that they use it primarily for word processing when, in fact, they use it primarily for playing video games.

potential adopters of personal computers). External validity is improved by randomly sampling respondents, by testing systems in a variety of natural settings, by involving respondents who represent target populations, and the like. Randomness is important for two reasons. First, it establishes the basis for the use of many statistical tests. Second, it guarantees that various rival hypotheses are not systematically likely, and thus tend to cancel each other out. The components of external validity include these concepts:

- Face validity: the reasonable operationalization of a proposed concept
- Predictive validity: the ability to predict future outcomes from a measurement
- Concurrent validity: association of a measure with conceptually similar variables
- Construct validity: a theoretic judgment of the degree to which an empirical measure fulfills the meaning of a concept's definition

The study of the new media may be particularly weak in face and construct validity because many new concepts and theories about the new media are not yet fully explicated. Validity is greatly influenced by the process of operationalization, the conversion of a concept into a variable by the explicit identification of aspects of the concept that will be used in the study and how they will be measured. In the following examples, we illustrate our present discussion of validity with recent research on the definition and measurement of the concepts of access to, and use of, the new media.

Access is the users' perceived ability to use a system to achieve his or her goal. It is an important determinant of both the use and evaluation of information in general, often more important then the utility, reliability, or quality of the information. With respect to new information systems, the concept of access is multidimensional. It includes physical access to a computer terminal, the availability of desired information through the system, the reliability of the system, and the ease of learning the control language to be able to use the new system (Culnan, 1984, 1985; Kerr & Hiltz, 1982; Rice and Shook, 1988).

Use of a new medium is the degree to which a user has experience with the medium. The concept of use may be operationalized in several ways, including duration (the total amount of time per day spent using a system), exposure (the number of days since the individual first used the system), and frequency (the number of times per day the individual logs on to the system; Chapter 6). A user may log on a system the first thing each morning and keep the computer on all day long for occasional work. In this case, duration of use is high but frequency of use is low. Or frequency may be high and duration low, perhaps indicating that the system is used just to check for received messages or to upload preprocessed text files. Frequency measures are likely to be most affected by difficulties of access. For instance, an individual might log on only a few times during the day because it is time-consuming to travel from one office to another to see if a computer terminal is free. Because access to this distant terminal is difficult, however, duration of use for each log-on may be longer than average. It is well to keep in mind that usage of a new medium is not the same as acceptance (the degree to which a user integrates a new medium into the range of communication choices for accomplishing goals), so that high levels of use do not necessarily mean a successful or beneficial system (Kerr & Hiltz, 1982).

The variety of measures that can be used to operationalize the concepts of access and use of a new medium allow for triangulation in the study of new media (Chapter 3).

RELIABILITY

Reliability is the degree to which a measure operationalizes a concept consistently over time and contexts. Reliability is analogous to the precision or consistency with which a dart thrower hits the same point on the target time after time. Reliability is necessary for validity, but not sufficient. A dart thrower may be consistent in missing the bull's-eye by the same amount each time, but will lose matches to an inconsistent opponent who also occasionally hits the bull's-eye. Traditional methods for determining reliability include computing test-retest intercorrelations by repeating or by giving two or more equivalent forms of the same measure to the same or similar respondents. It can also be estimated by comparing portions of the measure, such as items in a scale, with the total measure (such as by computing Cronbach's *alpha* between each item and the total score on a scale).

Validity and reliability are two criteria by which new scales are evaluated for use in research on the new media. Table 4–2 lists some scales, along with a representative question from each, that have

Table 4–2. Selected Scales and Examples for Use in Studying the New Media

1. Individual innovativeness (Hurt, Joseph & Cook, 1977): "I am challenged by ambiguities and unsolved problems."
2. Perceived organizational innovativeness (Hurt & Teigen, 1977): "The organization I work for seeks out new ways to do things." (Siegel & Kaemmerer, 1978): "Around here people are allowed to try to solve the same problem in different ways."
3. Microcomputer anxiety (Howard & Smith, 1986): "I hesitate to use a computer for fear of making mistakes that I cannot correct."
4. User information satisfaction (Ives et al., 1983): "The users' understanding of the system is . . . sufficient . . . insufficient; complete . . . incomplete."
5. Perceived usefulness of a system (Franz & Robey, 1986): "To what extent does this system assist you in performing your job better?"
6. Task routineness, complexity, variety, and amount (Withey et al., 1983): "To do your work, to what extent can you actually rely on established procedures and practices?"
7. Parasocial interaction (Rubin et al., 1985): "I would like to meet my favorite newscaster in person."

been developed according to procedures for establishing scale reliability and validity, and have been useful in studying aspects of the new media.

SAMPLING

Sampling is the selection of some subset of respondents or other objects of study from the relevant population of all such respondents or objects. A researcher may want to study only a subset instead of the entire population because it would be impractical (too costly, time-consuming, difficult to analyze, etc.) to collect data from *all* respondents. Often it is inefficient to study an entire population, even if it were possible, because the results from a much smaller but well-chosen sample will closely approximate the results from the total population.

As the example from Elton and Carey's teletext study noted, choices made in sampling design affect the external validity of a study's results by determining whether the research results can be generalized to other situations. For example, how would you evaluate the results from a study of children's motivations for playing videogames when the data were gathered from a group of six children leaving a videoarcade together? They probably did not have independent motivations, so a skewed distribution of motivations from this "sample" would result.

There are at least five specific ways in which sampling designs in the study of new media may affect internal and external validity and generalizability.

1. *The type of respondents or social system.* If only early adopters of a new medium are studied, the results of their attitudes toward that new medium may be atypical of the more general audience that represents the wider population of eventual users. Such a lack of generalizability contributed to the unrealistic market projections for videotext in the United States in the early 1980s. Results from a study of the use of communication technology in one country or cultural system may not be valid for one with different cultural norms concerning centralization, hierarchical control of information, and symbolic value of technology (Mody, 1985). Indeed, for studies of certain new media at a very early stage of diffusion, it is difficult to find a sample of users large enough to analyze by means of multivariate statistical procedures.

2. *The strategy used in sampling respondents.* A nonprobability sample may reduce the external validity of a study. For example, a trade magazine may report an evaluation of personal computers based on responses to a questionnaire mailed to names on the magazine's subscription list. Not only may these respondents fail to be a relevant audience for understanding what differentiates adopters from non-adopters, but certain subscribers are more likely to respond to the survey because they have a favorable attitude toward the new medium.

3. *The type of new communication technology.* Many studies of office automation have failed either to specify the exact nature of the computer system that is studied or to compare it to other possible configurations of the computer system. The results of such studies are not generalizable to other kinds of integrated office systems (Jarven-paa et al., 1986; Kerr & Hiltz, 1982).

4. *The time period.* Problems in generalizing across time are illustrated by many past studies that show that attitudes, usage, and reported outcomes vary considerably between the first few months of use of a new medium and a year or so later (Hiltz & Turoff, 1981).

5. *The use of sampling itself.* Many adopters of a new medium such as electronic mail use it to communicate with a specific set of other individuals in a social system; therefore, a random sample contradicts the interdependencies among individuals that the new medium makes possible (this is the "critical mass" of adoptors discussed in Chapter 5). Also, a new medium that connects geographically and temporally dispersed users is revealed through network analysis, which requires a census instead of a sample (Chapter 11).

In all, the ways in which respondents or objects of study are sampled greatly influences the validity, and subsequent usefulness, of studies of the new media.

What sampling designs can be used to ensure validity in new media studies?

Random sampling guarantees that each unit in a population has an equal probability of being selected in the sample. A random sample may be used to eliminate possible error or bias. An example is the random assignment of individuals to computer-mediated or face-to-face decision-making groups so that prior preferences for (or familiarity with) the new media are not unexpectedly concentrated in either experimental group.

Stratified sampling consists of drawing a sample from each of several categories (strata) of a total population. Stratification is used to guarantee that variance in different variables is measured, such as sampling from urban and rural adopters of videocassette recorders, or that different influences are removed from a study, such as sampling only users of a new medium to avoid including responses by people who are not familiar with the medium. The first guarantees that the proper independent variables are measured, while the second guarantees that possible intervening variables are either measured or removed.

Disproportionate sampling consists of drawing a sample from each of several categories of a total population at sampling rates that are not proportionate to their numbers in the total population. For example, in its sample of U.S. households, Nielsen, Inc., oversamples the number of Blacks and Hispanics asked to complete television viewing diaries so that the final sample sizes by race are proportionate to the number of these viewers in the U.S. population; this is necessary because minorities are more difficult to enlist in Nielsen diary studies. A more common example of disproportionate stratified sampling occurs when one or more strata are oversampled because of special interest in the behavior of these individuals.

Cluster sampling consists of drawing groupings of several respondents together as a sampling unit. Cluster sampling is used to reduce the cost and time involved in collecting data. For example, researchers might study the use of computers by elementary school students in several local schools within the same school district instead of randomly selecting students from all elementary schools across the nation. Each school district is a cluster in this illustration.

Studying the New Media Over Time

NEED FOR A TEMPORAL PERSPECTIVE

Research that studies new media at one time—cross-sectional studies—must be concerned with issues of validity, reliability, and sampling. Studies of new media over time place greater demands on these elements of research, but also have the opportunity of increasing the validity and reliability of the results.

The new media are part of human activities, and they must fit, over time, into existing patterns of media consumption as well as people's expectations about possible benefits and disadvantages of using the new medium. Also, the new media themselves change over time. Personal computers, videocassette players, and compact disks change each year in terms of price, technical capabilities, and ease of use. Political and social contexts of media change over time as well. Thus, the main assumption of cross-sectional research designs—that the system being analyzed is stable—is low in external validity in the case of the new media. We recommend that researchers studying new media use theories, designs, and methods that take change over time into account in order to improve the meaningfulness of their results and to capture the social dynamics of the new media.

Following are examples of the advantages of studying new media over time:

- To identify and track changes such as shifts in attitudes toward a new communication system (Hiltz & Turoff, 1981)
- To model how patterns of interactions among individuals using a computer conferencing system develop (Rice, 1982)
- To understand the political forces at different stages in implementing a municipal information system (Dutton, 1981)
- To understand better how personal computers in the home fit into the preexisting media environment (Vitalari et al., 1985)
- To develop a processual model of diffusion to forecast the acquisition of new computer terminals for use by engineers (Randles, 1983)

CHOICES IN OVER-TIME RESEARCH

Selection of the most appropriate analytical method for the study of change over time is guided by:

- The number of measurement points
- The overall length of the study in time
- Whether the same respondents are analyzed at each time point (a panel study), different respondents are used (pooled cross-sectional time-series), or whether different respondents at the same stage of use are analyzed (a cohort study)
- Whether the order, magnitude, or total of certain variables at each time period is used as a variable (a temporal study)
- Whether the rate of change across time periods is used as a variable (a dynamic study)
- Whether values at one time period must be corrected for values

at previous time periods (statistical control of autocorrelation in time-series and multistage multiple regression)
• Whether univariate (trend) or multivariate (simultaneous) equations are used

A variety of research methods are available for studying the new media over time. For instance, a case study provides a narrative analysis of a process, ideally according to a theoretical framework, such as a typology of actors, influences, and consequences (Chapter 7). A case study may follow a historical approach, analyzing legal documents and participants' recall of events, such as the implementation of an interactive cable television system in a community (Dutton, Blumler & Kraemer, 1987). Or a case study may involve "participant observation," such as a researcher's becoming part of a computer bulletin board users' group to analyze the interactions of an on-line community.

Certain statistical methods can test hypotheses about time-ordered relationships among variables that are measured at several points in time. For example, partial correlation and structural equation models have been used to test two alternate models. Attitudes about a computer communication system influence usage levels, which in turn influence outcomes, or usage influences attitudes, which then influence perceived outcomes. If the partial correlations (or standardized regression coefficients) between attitudes and usage, and between usage and outcomes, are significantly different from zero, while those between attitudes and outcomes are not significantly different from zero, then the first model is more strongly supported than the second.

Statistical methods may be used to test differences in variables between two time periods. A researcher interested in the effect of a "hands-on" demonstration of an electronic news service on potential adopters' perceived attributes of this innovation might use a simple t-test to compare the average perceived relative advantage of the service before, and after, the demonstration. Differences in the means of all five dimensions of perceived innovation attributes (Chapter 5) before, and after, a demonstration can be simultaneously tested with Hotelling's T-square, which controls for the interdependence of the five dimensions. Or, a communications scholar might use canonical correlation to determine the degree to which the multiple dimensions on which the new medium is perceived before the demonstration are similar to the dimensions that are perceived afterward. Other statistical methods for comparing changes in variables across two or more time periods include cross-lagged correlation, repeated measures analysis of variance, N-way dimensional scaling, pooled cross-sectional time-series, time-series, and Markov analysis.[1]

Problems in Studying New Media Over Time

Why are there so few over-time studies of the new media? One reason is the usually substantial cost and effort expended in collecting such data. There is also the possibility that the new media (or other issues of study) will not be considered as important (or may not exist in comparable form) by the time the study is completed. Then, too, difficulties typically arise in recruiting and keeping respondents. There are always special challenges in selecting the appropriate measurement intervals, and the proper statistical methods are not as well known. There are usually long delays between starting the study and providing the research results. The cumulative effect on the respondents of repeated surveys, interviews, and observation sometimes causes major problems, too. And finally, there is a relative lack of theory about processes involving change over time.

Some of these problems can be lessened by focusing on more enduring issues, by collecting larger samples than needed initially, by producing progress reports at reasonable intervals, by comparing user groups to nonuser control groups, by incorporating archival temporal or dynamic variables in cross-sectional analyses, or by randomly selecting a small set of individuals to provide responses to a few questions frequently.

The difficulty of conducting over-time analysis of the new media has meant that there are only a few such studies. However, a few examples follow.

Several studies have combined cross-sectional questionnaire data with over-time computer-monitored system usage data (Chapter 6). If these data include when the system began and when each user first logged on to the system, the researcher can conduct temporal analyses of change in usage over time and the influence of different lengths of use of the new media system. Such studies may show that the use of a new medium is decreasing over time despite reported positive attitudes toward, or benefits from, respondents' use of the new medium.

Rice (1982) analyzed the message links among nearly 800 users of a nationwide computer conferencing system during its first two years of use. Data measuring interaction among users were aggregated into twenty-four one-month periods and into ten groups of users. A longitudinal analysis of the communication roles of carriers, transmitters, receivers, and isolates were carried out for each of the twenty-four time periods so that trends across time could be identified. Groups that had a specific goal or task to accomplish using the conferencing system generally became and remained isolates, while groups that were invited to use the system to explore its appropriateness for communication among researchers tended to shift from transmitter or receiver roles to carriers. A later analysis of these same data used dynamic variables derived from "Galileo," a multidimensional scaling program that can statistically control for prior network patterns in a series of networks over time (Rice & Barnett, 1986). The dynamic analysis showed that new groups disrupted the network's stability when they entered the computer conferencing system, but the overall network soon returned to a stable structure.

Gutek (1982) investigated the interactions, attitudes, and reported benefits of a single manager-secretary dyad as they used an integrated computer workstation. Quantitative and qualitative data were collected every two weeks for a two-year period: before the pair received the workstation, during its use, and after the workstation was removed. The data from fifty time-periods were analyzed to determine changes in the psychological environments of the dyad. Although there was little change in behaviors over the two years (except that telephone use increased after the computer system was removed), there was considerable change in attitudes. For example, the secretary reported the least creative work before the office system was installed; both secretary and manager reported less complex work before installation, and the manager felt more organized after installation of the workstation.

Summary

Researchers interested in studying the new media must confront serious challenges to validity and reliability. Because new media are parts of complex social systems, it is important to study them in natural settings. Research designs that increase external validity (conventional designs such as field experiments and interpretive designs such as participant observation) also make it more difficult to achieve satisfactory internal validity. Researchers need to explore a wider range of alternatives and to be more explicit about the possible biases or limitations of the research design used in a given study.

Because new media often represent novel and unique situations that are not yet well understood, researchers have to satisfy opposing demands for reliability and validity. On the one hand, reliable measures are needed to remove as much measurement error as possible from a situation that is filled with ambiguity and possible misinterpretation. On the other hand, measures developed to study prior relationships may prevent the researcher from discovering new relationships. Again, researchers studying new media must consider these trade-offs and make them explicit in their reports.

Finally, it is clear that the study of new media requires the use of theories, methods, and designs that explicitly consider change over time. Actually, nearly all the topics of communication research require this approach. New media studies should use a variety of methodological alternatives to develop over-time research that is based on this understanding right from the start.

Note

1. The reader interested in learning how to apply longitudinal methods of analysis in communication research should turn to specialized sources on this topic (Monge & Cappella, 1980).

CHAPTER 5

Adoption of New Media

The Importance of Interactivity

The purpose of this chapter is to explore one special quality of the new media, "interactivity," that affects the rate of adoption of these innovations, with emphasis on the research methods used to study this issue.

The general theory of the diffusion of innovations can be applied to the adoption and use of interactive media. Diffusion is the process by which an innovation is communicated through certain channels over time among the members of a social system (Rogers, 1983). The new communication technologies are distinctive in their degree of interactivity (Chapter 1), which may uniquely influence their rate of adoption in organizations. Electronic mail and computer bulletin boards are two examples of interactive media. Unlike many other innovations that have been studied in past diffusion investigations, interactive media require that a "critical mass" of adopters begin using the innovation before its S-shaped curve of diffusion takes off. The rate of adoption for interactive media is expected to be slower than for noninteractive innovations in the early stages, but then to increase rapidly.

What Is the Diffusion Paradigm?

The main elements in the diffusion of new ideas are: (1) an innovation, (2) which is communicated through certain channels, (3) over time, (4) among the members of a social system (Figure 5–1). An innovation is an idea, practice, or object perceived as new by an individual or other unit of adoption (Rogers, 1983). The characteristics of an innovation, as perceived by the members of a social system, determine its rate of adoption. Five attributes of innovations are: (1) relative advantage, (2) compatibility, (3) complexity, (4) trialability, and (5) observability.

Mass media channels of communication are usually more effective in creating awareness-knowledge of innovations, whereas interpersonal channels are more effective in forming, and in changing, attitudes toward a new idea, and thus indirectly influencing the decision to adopt or reject a new idea. Most individuals evaluate an innovation that they are considering adopting, not because of scientific research by experts, but through the subjective evaluations of near-peers who have previously adopted the innovation.

Time is involved throughout the diffusion process, including in:

1. The *innovation-decision* process, the mental process through which an individual or other decision-making unit passes from first knowledge of an innovation to forming an attitude toward

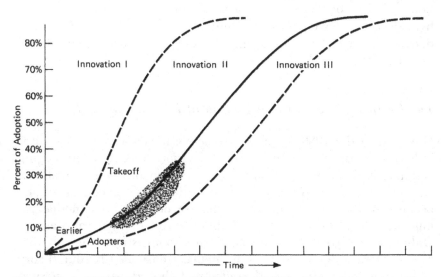

Figure 5–1. Diffusion Is the Process by Which (1) an Innovation (2) Is Communicated Through Certain Channels (3) Over Time (4) Among the Members of a Social System

SOURCE: Everett M. Rogers, *Diffusion of Innovations*, 3rd Ed. (New York: The Free Press, 1983), p. 11. Copyright © 1983 by The Free Press, a Division of Macmillan Publishing Co., Inc. Used by permission.

the innovation, to a decision to adopt or reject, to implementation of the new idea, and to confirmation of this decision.
2. *Innovativeness*, the degree to which an individual or other unit of adoption is earlier in adopting new ideas than other members of a social system.
3. An innovation's *rate of adoption*, the relative speed with which an innovation is adopted by members of a social system.

Figure 5–1 shows innovations with a more rapid, and with a slower, rate of adoption. The most frequently studied issue in diffusion research is to determine factors related to the level of adoption by individuals.

A social system is a set of interrelated units that are engaged in joint problem-solving to accomplish a common goal. The units in a system may be individuals, organizations, families, or nations. A system has structure, the patterned arrangements of the units in a system, and this structure provides regularity and predictability to behavior in a system. The four main elements in diffusion, the key definitions of concepts, and the relationships among these conceptual variables constitute the diffusion paradigm. It grew gradually out of empirical investigations, which pointed to the regularities of innovation diffusion behavior across a wide variety of innovations (e.g., hybrid corn, snowmobiles, and microcomputers), types of respondents (e.g., farmers, doctors, managers of organizations), and in different contexts.

The Critical Mass in the Adoption of Interactive Media

Diffusion in the 1980s of such interactive media as microcomputer bulletin boards, interactive cable television, electronic messaging systems, and teleconferencing display certain distinctive qualities. One of the most important is the "critical mass" aspect, especially because of the special interactive nature of these new media. An innovation is of little use to an individual unless others also adopt. Only in recent years have scholars begun to investigate the adoption of the interactive communication media. Consequently, our theory and methods for studying the effects of the critical mass in such diffusion is limited.

A critical mass of adopters of an interactive communication medium is necessary for the utility of the new idea to be sufficient for an individual to adopt. The usefulness of a new communication system increases for all adopters with each additional adopter. An extreme illustration is provided by the first individual to adopt a telephone in the 1870s. This interactive technology had zero utility until a second individual adopted. The lack of a critical mass early in the diffusion process is a negative influence, slowing the rate of adoption (Figure 5–2).

The idea of a critical mass originated in physics, where it was defined as the amount of radioactive material that was necessary to produce a nuclear explosion. For human social behavior, a critical mass is "a small segment of the population that chooses to make big contributions to the collective action while the majority do little or nothing" (Oliver et al., 1985). The early adopters of an interactive medium make this contribution to the system by evaluating the new technology.

Much of the theory and research concerning the critical mass in recent decades was inspired by Mancur Olson's (1965, p. 2) "logic of collective action":

> Even if all the individuals in a large group are rational and self-in-terested, and would gain if, as a group, they acted to achieve their common interest or objective, they would still not voluntarily act to achieve that common or group interest.

Why is individual behavior in a large group so illogical? The basic reason is that each individual acts in ways that seem rational in pursu-

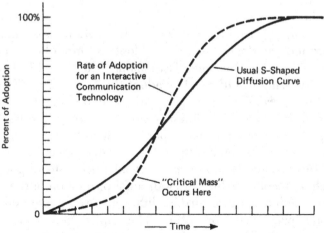

Figure 5–2. The Rate of Adoption (1) for the Usual Innovation, and (2) for an Interactive Communication Technology, Showing the "Critical Mass"

ing individual goals without fully considering that the individual is disadvantaging himself or herself (and others in the system) at the collective level. For example, consider that a new electronic messaging system is introduced in an organization. Someone obviously has to adopt first, but the first adopter cannot communicate with any other member of the organization until a second individual has adopted. And, of course, adoption of the electronic messaging system has greater and greater utility for each user as more and more individuals adopt. But if the first adopters only think of their own benefits at the time they adopt (rather than thinking about what may eventually be to their benefit, or what may be beneficial for their organization), no one would adopt. Until there is a critical mass of adopters, an interactive communication system has little advantage (and considerable disadvantage) for each adopter.

Professor M. Lynne Markus (1987) has advanced theoretical understanding of the role of the critical mass in the diffusion of interactive media. She points out that the key question in understanding the role of the critical mass in diffusion is why an individual adopts an interactive medium at the early stages of diffusion. Perhaps an individual may decide to adopt on the basis of an anticipation that the innovation's adoption is likely to takeoff when peers adopt. However, most individuals do not adopt an innovation until they learn of their peers' successful experience with a new idea. Prior to formation of the critical mass, any given individual adopter is unlikely to have such peers who have already adopted.

The notion of the critical mass calls for important modifications of diffusion theory in the particular case of interactive technologies. The formulation may also apply to such other innovations as clothing fashions where independence among the adopters cannot be assumed. A new item of clothing becomes fashionable when a critical mass of elites start wearing it. Others then adopt the new fashion. There is a good deal of interdependence among the adopters of all innovations in the sense of an adopter influencing peers to adopt the innovation by telling them about a positive experience with the innovation. This peer influence is what makes the diffusion curve takeoff somewhere between the 5 percent and 20 percent adoption rate (Figure 5–1). Once such a takeoff is achieved, additional promotion of the innovation is not needed because further diffusion is self-generated by the innovation's own social momentum. This explanation, again, sounds like a "critical mass" concept. What is different in the special case of interactive technologies is that there is a built-in "forcing quality" in the adopter-to-decider relationship. "It takes two to tango," Katz (1962) has pointed out.

Research is needed to identify the "tipping point" at which a critical mass begins to propel the rate of diffusion in a way that is self-generating and nonreversible (Granovetter, 1978). Mathematically, this point is the inflection at which the diffusion curve begins to increase at an increasing rate (defined as occurring at 16 percent adoption, one standard deviation before the mean time of adoption in a system). However, this mathematical formulation may only be a rough approximation. If the purpose of such research is to identify the point of takeoff in the rate of adoption, such research need not be limited to interactive innovations. It could be an important question for any innovation research to pursue. The stakes here may be grander than for just exploring what modifications are needed in the diffusion model for interactive innovations.

Some preliminary research on the effects of the critical mass on adoption of interactive communication systems has been conducted by Rice, Grant, Schmitz, and Torobin (1988). Taking a network approach (see Chapter 11), they have shown that (1) the extent of an individual's communication with other members in a small organization *before* the implementation of an electronic messaging system was a very positive influence on one's *later* adoption of the system, and (2) the extent of an individual's communication with other adopters *after* implementation was a very positive influence on the extent to which the respondent reported positive benefits from using the system. The first influence indicates that a critical mass of others with whom one communicates makes it more likely that an individual will use such a system, and the second influence indicates that a critical mass of other users increases the perceived utility of the new communication system.

Finally, a key question to be answered in future research is who is in the critical mass of adopters? What are the characteristics of these individuals? Are they individuals who are motivated by altruism or by future expectations to adopt at a time prior to that at which the maximum benefits from an interactive innovation will be secured?

Adoption of Computer-Mediated Communication Systems

A useful example of an interactive communication medium is a computer bulletin board that allows private electronic messaging (some bulletin boards do not). Individuals can communicate directly with any other participant who is connected to the same computer bulletin board. Each of these communities of individuals shares a common interest in some topic. Such a computer network has a minimum of social structure that might shape communication flows, so that a computer bulletin board approaches a communication free-for-all. These electronic networks are highly interactive in that they closely approach human conversations in nature (with the important difference that all messages have to be typed into a computer keyboard). Although the percentage of the U.S. population that belongs to at least one computer bulletin board is low (probably only 1 percent or 2 percent), the number of bulletin boards has increased rapidly during the 1980s.

A computer bulletin board consists of a host computer that is accessed by participants using their own terminal and/or microcomputer connected to the network by telephone lines. A special software package is needed at the host computer to route the message traffic. A bulletin board is much like a local area network or an electronic messaging system in an organization, except that the bulletin board is a communication system usually with an open membership. Any individual who shares a common interest (e.g., anti-nuclear warfare, computer music, gay liberation) with other participants on the bulletin board is welcome to join, usually by just dialing a particular telephone number. The participants post notices, make requests for help, and take part in an ongoing discussion of some topic.

Presumably, message exchange via computer bulletin boards can provide an extremely democratic communication system. Each individual has direct access through the electronic network to every other member of the bulletin board. The communication system is "destatused" in that there is no social or organizational hierarchy. Gatekeeping, such as by a receptionist or secretary, is absent because most members of a computer bulletin board process their own electronic mail (Sproull & Kiesler, 1986). Perhaps it is surprising that under these conditions participation in such interactive systems is not equal. A common research finding is that about 50 percent of all messages are sent by only about 10 percent of the participants.

In general, electronic mail systems have many of the characteristics of computer bulletin boards, but they are used primarily by members of a single organization. Some electronic mail systems are large in size. For example, the Hewlett-Packard Company has an electronic messaging system for transmitting information among its various plants and sales offices. The average cost is only about one cent per hundred-word message for domestic transmission, which compares favorably with the cost of a first-class stamp in the United States (Pool, 1983b, pp. 190–191). The Hewlett-Packard system carries about 25 million messages per year among its 45,000 employees.

In an interactive communication system like an electronic messaging system, bypassing of the layers in the organizational hierarchy may occur, especially during the early stages of the system's use. Participants send many copies of a message to their colleagues, in part because it is so easy to do. Such electronic messaging behavior can lead to information overload. Most organizations ordinarily forbid an employee to communicate directly with the boss's boss, thus bypassing the direct supervisor. When an electronic messaging system is first provided in an organization, there is often a tendency to bypass this hierarchy. Participants, especially executives, soon begin to complain about being overloaded with messages. Gradually, over a period of several months, this problem is resolved as participants learn to be more sparing in sending electronic carbon copies of their messages.

We can see an example of the usual sequence that occurs in the diffusion process of an interactive medium like a computer bulletin board or an electronic messaging system. The system of users gradually learn from their own and others' experience with the innovation, so initial problems such as bypassing and overload are overcome. If they do not, the new medium fails. Particularly important in how members of the system gradually learn about the advantages and disadvantages of the interactive medium is the critical mass of early adopters.

Implications of the Critical Mass Concept for Research Methods

If one acknowledges that the critical mass is involved in the adoption of an interactive medium, how should diffusion research on these innovations differ from past studies of noninteractive technologies? An ideal study of an interactive innovation might well include:

- Data from a sample of systems (like organizations adopting electronic messaging systems) in which the same interactive innovation was diffusing
- Microlevel data from individuals in each system of study con-

cerning their adoption decisions and use of the interactive innovation (validated with computer-monitored data about adoption
and use)
• Data over time concerning the diffusion process of the interactive innovation
• Network measures to show the paths of influence in a social
system and the extent of critical mass for each individual

Past diffusion research, focusing mainly on individual innovativeness, contrasts sharply with this ideal study. It is almost as if
past diffusion research had been perfectly designed not to focus on
the critical mass in the diffusion of an interactive communication
innovation. Perhaps this shortcoming is because most social science
research methods assume that the phenomena of study are independent. An example is the assumption that the individuals adopting an
innovation are not interrelated with one another. This faulty assumption of independence grows out of the fact that individuals are often
the unit of response in statistical analyses, so their interactions are
overlooked. As Wellman (1983, p. 160) has noted, "The Statistical
Package for the Social Sciences became a world view." Unfortunately,
this is a view devoid of network relationships.

We feel that an important improvement in adoption research lies
in the study of a person's network relationships with other individuals
in order to explain that individual's adoption of a new medium (Chapter 11). As explained previously in this chapter, past diffusion studies
emphasize that most people adopt an innovation when the individual's peers have adopted and conveyed to others their satisfaction
with the new idea. So the adoption of an innovation is a social behavior. That much is known. But the microlevel network behavior
through which such interpersonal influence occurs has not been adequately studied to date.

A next research step lies in a careful network analysis of the
person-to-person spread of an interactive innovation among the members of a system. Here, network analysis can be "an extra set of
variables added on like a turbocharter to boost the explained variance" in the dependent variable of innovativeness (Wellman, 1983, p.
133). The recommended research approach is to determine how
much variance in the dependent variable of innovativeness (the relative time-of-adoption of an innovation) is explained by nonnetwork
variables, such as the personal and social characteristics of individuals
adopting an innovation. Next is to determine how much additional

variance in the dependent variable of innovativeness is explained by the "turbocharger" of network variables, like the number of an individuals' peers who have already adopted the innovation of study. Chapter 11 provides a detailed example of such turbocharger network research on innovativeness in adopting a computer-based hospital information system.

Forecasting the Diffusion of New Media

AN EMPHASIS ON PREDICTION

Most past diffusion research attempted to understand the rate of adoption of an innovation after its diffusion was largely completed so as to derive general principles about factors affecting relatively slower and more rapid rates of adoption. In contrast, another research approach is to forecast the rate of adoption of an innovation before its diffusion has occurred so as to predict the likely rate of adoption. Such forecasts can be useful, if they are accurate. Here we focus on three questions:

1. How accurate are the forecasts for the adoption of the new media?
2. How is the rate of adoption forecast?
3. Why are certain forecasting methods more accurate, or more useful, for the new media?

Following are some examples in studies of new media.

THE FAILURE OF VIDEODISC PLAYERS

In April 1984, RCA announced that it was discontinuing its videodisc player, taking a loss of $580 million. Only about 550,000 Selectavision players had been sold (at $500 each) over a three-year period. A videodisc is a kind of marriage of videotape and microcomputer technology. The disk itself looks like an LP record. It is "read" by a laser beam in the player equipment. The microcomputer element means that random access of the contents of a disk is possible. The sound and video quality are excellent. RCA conducted extensive prelaunch research and advertised its product heavily. What went wrong?

Bruce C. Klopfenstein (1986), a communication scholar at Bowling Green State University, identified several key factors in the failure of videodisc players. Most important was competition from a similar product, videocassette recorders (VCRs), which dropped in price sharply during the 1981–84 period, thus destroying RCA's main advertising claim that the videodisc player was inexpensive. Further, only a limited number of videodiscs were available, and they cost from $20 to $30 (much more than videotapes). A further advantage of the VCR was that it would record at home from television broadcasts or copy other tapes, while the videodisc player could only play back prerecorded disks. While RCA conducted market research in order to forecast the rate of adoption of the videdisc players, "no demonstrated need for a home video playback-only device had been shown" (Klopfenstein, 1986).

The expensive failure of RCA's videodisc player also represented a failure in forecasting the product's rate of adoption and in identifying how potential adopters perceived the characteristics of this interactive innovation.

CENTERS OF FORECASTING RESEARCH

A few university scholars plus a handful of nonprofit research centers are involved in forecasting the rate of adoption for the new media. Examples are:

- The Institute for the Future, Menlo Park, California, a nonprofit research institute that is mainly supported by an annual membership fee as well as funding by large companies
- The Future of the Mass Audience Project at the Massachusetts Institute of Technology, which operates an Audience Research Facility in the Liberty Tree Mall in Danvers, Massachusetts and is funded by ABC, Ampex, Home Box Office, RCA, 3M, Time, Warner Communications, Polaroid, GTE, the New York Times, and the Washington Post (This field laboratory provides the MIT investigators with a convenient, continuous supply of respondents who are asked to provide data about their use of, and perceptions of, the new media.)

The fact that these organizations are funded primarily by corporate sponsors in the communication industry often means that the research results can only be disseminated to the scholarly community after a considerable delay if at all. In addition to the commercial researchers and university scholars who conduct technology assessments of the new media, such government agencies as the National Science Foundation and the Office of Technology Assessment (OTA) are also involved in technology forecasting.

How Accurate Are Forecasts?

The main variable that is usually forecast for the new media is their rate of adoption—that is, the relative speed with which an innovation is adopted by members of a system. When the number of U.S. households adopting such new media as VCRs and microcomputers is plotted on a cumulative frequency over time, the resulting distribution usually approaches an S-shaped curve (as was shown in Figure 5–1). At first, only a few households purchase the new medium during each time period (e.g., a year). Soon the diffusion curve begins to climb as more and more households adopt per time period. Eventually, the rate of adoption begins to level off, and fewer and fewer households remain who have not yet adopted. Finally, the S-shaped curve reaches its asymptote, and the diffusion process is completed (although discontinuance or re-invention can occur afterward).

The Future of the Mass Audience Project has developed a microcomputer system called MEDIACALC, which forecasts the rate of adoption of the new media. MEDIACALC is an integrated model in that fifty-four communication technologies are included, allowing a forecaster to analyze trade-offs between a technology that is widely diffused and one that is just emerging (e.g., television versus videocassette recorders). Figure 5–3 shows a MEDIACALC projection for the rate of adoption of VCRs that is based on optimistic assumptions about this new technology. About 85 percent of U.S. households are predicted to eventually own a VCR. When less optimistic assumptions are made, such as that competitive means of transmitting movies to the home will develop, only 60 percent of U.S. households are predicted to adopt.

The diffusion scenario described previously is a fairly accurate description of the rate of adoption of black-and-white televisions in the United States (Figure 5–3). This S-curve may also fit other new media that are presently in the process of diffusing in the United States. Or it may not. A new medium may start off with a rapid rate of diffusion, but die completely before 1 percent or 2 percent adoption is reached (such as with the RCA videodisc example described ear-

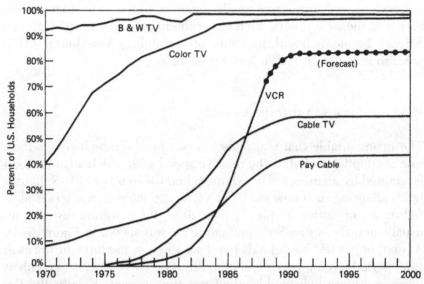

Figure 5–3. Actual and Forecast Rates of Adoption for Black-and-White Television, Color Television, Cable Television, Videocassette Recorders, and Pay Cable Television

SOURCE: MEDIACALC forecasts made by the MIT Future of the Mass Audience Project, with optimistic assumptions for VCR diffusion; used by permission.

lier). Or the rate of adoption may follow a complete S-shaped curve, but it is one that levels off at 35 percent, or 45 percent, or 50 percent of all U.S. households, as has been predicted for home computers. Or the rate of adoption may reach almost 100 percent of all U.S. households, but the diffusion process may progress much more slowly, or rapidly, than for black-and-white TV (which took ten to twelve years for most U.S. households to adopt). As Figure 5–3 shows, cable television has diffused much more slowly than black-and-white television. In contrast, the rate of adoption for compact disks (CDs) in the 1980s seems to be off to an even more rapid start than for black-and-white television in the 1950s. So the slope of the S-curve varies from one new medium to another, with some new communication technologies diffusing rapidly and others more slowly.

Big stakes can be involved in making accurate forecasts of communication technology adoption, and considerable effort is devoted to this important task. A corporation wants to know how rapidly or slowly a market will develop for the new communication technology that it has developed. Government and other planners want to anticipate the future rate of adoption for a new medium so they can prepare for the social impacts that will occur. A subcommittee of the U.S. Congress has been concerned with the diffusion of microcomputers to U.S. households and whether this technology is widening the gap between the information-rich and the information-poor.

How accurate are forecasts for the rate of adoption of new communication media? We can determine such accuracy by comparing a forecast made at t_1 (time one) for the rate of adoption of a new medium at t_2 (time two) with the rate of adoption that actually happened by t_2. When this type of procedure is followed, we often find that such forecasts are inaccurate. Here are some examples:

- The telephone was originally developed by Alexander Graham Bell as an aid for the deaf. Somewhat later, the telephone was expected to serve as a carrier of entertainment services (such as live band music) into the home (Pool, 1983a), thus fulfilling the function of a modern radio.
- Parker (1973b) predicted that in twelve years, by 1985, cable television would reach 85 percent of U.S. households. The figure in 1985 turned out to be about half of that predicted.
- In 1980, it was forecast that 500,000 videocassette recorders would be sold in 1985, a considerable underestimate for the much more rapid rate of adoption that actually occurred in 1985 (when sales were closer to 8 million units). VCRs in 1980 were expected to be used for playing back prerecorded materials, much like home stereo music systems; the time-shifting use of VCRs was not forecast.
- In 1986, Knight-Ridder's Viewtron and Times-Mirror's Gateway, two expensive videotext trials, failed in Florida and California, respectively. The Knight-Ridder newspaper chain had invested about $60 million in their Viewtron project, which had 21,000 subscribers at its peak. So this technology prediction, made in the early 1980s, was optimistically inaccurate and expensive.
- When Prestel, the videotext service provided by British Telecommunications, began for-profit operation in 1979, 2 million households were forecast to adopt by the end of 1981. Instead, by May 1984, there were only 36,000 adopters, of which only 11,000 were households (the remainder were business users). By 1984, there were about half a million videotext users worldwide (in nineteen countries). The Institute for the Future predicted

there would be 11 million videotext users by 1990; by 1986, there were only about 600,000.

• An early forecast estimated that half a dozen mainframe computers would be sufficient for all the computing needs in the United States. These forecasters were thinking only in terms of mainframe computers, of course; they did not anticipate the proliferation of microcomputers in the late 1970s. By 1987, about 20 percent of U.S. households (over 16 million) had adopted microcomputers.

How Is the Rate of Adoption Forecast?

Most conventional social science data-gathering methods function best as rearview mirrors rather than as means to look into future behavior. For example, a survey of users of a new communication medium can indicate who has adopted the innovation (and thus who has not) and their degree of satisfaction with the new medium. This information may be useful in making predictions about the further rate of adoption of the innovation, but the survey of users obviously cannot be carried out until there are a number of such adopters. Forecasts of the diffusion rate for a new technology are most valuable before it has any adopters.

The general point here is that all the methods of forecasting suffer difficulties in attempting to provide data about a future that has not yet occurred. However, the situation is not completely hopeless. Even in the previous example of the user survey, certain valuable information can be learned. Methodological advances in recent years make technological forecasting a more accurate activity than previously. The best forecasts are based on a triangulation of data-gathering methods, each of which can provide certain useful information (Chapter 3).

What are some of the most widely used methods of forecasting the rate of adoption for a new communication medium? Following are the major methods.

Delphi method. This forecasting technique, named for the Oracle at Delphi in ancient Greece, uses the consensus of a panel of experts on the particular topic at hand (e.g., a new medium) and typically proceeds in sequential rounds of responses from the panel. At each round, the panel's previous responses are fed back to the experts on an anonymous basis, and the previous forecasts are then modified.

Thus, the Delphi method may proceed through a sequence of several gradual approximations. This forecasting method functions most effectively when the members of the panel of experts each possess knowledge about a certain aspect of the forecast to be made, without overlapping the other experts, so that the pooling of opinions adds up to a multifaceted forecast. Turoff (1978) provides a useful description of Delphi procedures.

Extrapolation from past rates of adoption. To the extent that regularities occur in the rates of adoption for various communication technologies, a new medium's S-curve may be predicted by extrapolating from a similar, past technology. An example is MIT's MEDIACALC system, which operates on the assumption of regularities in rates of adoption (Figure 5–3). MEDIACALC allows the researcher forecasting the rate of adoption for a new technology to assume it may diffuse similarly to an older medium. Will the rate of adoption of CDs be more similar to black-and-white television, color television, or cable television?

As we discussed in Chapter 2, communication scholars have investigated the effects of a single new medium (radio, television, or computers, for example), but have seldom compared one communication technology with another, or explored the impact of one medium on another. For example, how did the widespread adoption of television in the United States during the 1950s change the nature of radio? How did children's use of computers in the 1980s compare with children's use of television since the 1950s?

Chen's study of computers in the lives of children was enriched by comparison with past research on children and television. For example, Chen (1984, p. 281) concluded: "Television research on TV violence and advertising looks at the child under a media effects paradigm. . . . But with computers the child is portrayed as a thinking child." Although Chen presented the S-shaped curves for television's diffusion among U.S. households in the 1950s, and for the rate of adoption of microcomputers among U.S. schools in the 1980s, he did not seek to forecast the latter from the former.

Is the adoption of one new communication medium by a household related to the adoption of other new media? The answer from research is generally "yes," but with some reservations. For example, Reagan (1987) gathered data from 279 households in Spokane, Washington, on the adoption of four technologies: cable TV, videotext, home computers, and VCRs. These new media were at different levels of adoption, with 53 percent of households having adopted cable TV, 28 percent VCRs, 15 percent home computers, and only 2 percent adopting videotext. Households adopting one of the four new media tended to have adopted the others, too. For example, 81 percent of videotext users had a microcomputer, compared to only 16 percent of nonusers of videotext. The personal and social characteristics of adopters of each of the four innovations were generally similar; for example, higher income characterized adopters of cable TV, VCRs, and home computers.

The perceived attributes of the new medium (such as its relative advantage over existing practice, compatibility, complexity, trialability, and observability) may serve as dimensions on which a new medium is compared with already-diffused media to forecast the new medium's rate of adoption (Rogers, 1983).

Concept testing. A written statement or a graphic representation of a new medium is provided to possible users of a new medium, who are then questioned about their likelihood of adoption, favorability toward the new idea, and their other perceptions. Sometimes concept testing is done in focus groups, small discussion groups of six to ten individuals who meet with a facilitator who leads their discussion to obtain in-depth understandings (Chapter 3). An obvious shortcoming with concept testing as a means of forecasting a new medium's future rate of adoption is the hypothetical nature of the stimulus. A picture or a sentence describing a computer, for example, hardly substitutes for experience with the real thing.

Pilot project. A new medium is tested on a trial basis among a selected set of users from whom data are then gathered about its use, satisfaction with, and perceptions of. For useful lessons to be learned from a pilot project, it should be carried out under realistic conditions so the results can be generalized. When the new media (e.g., electronic messaging systems) are piloted in a large organization, the pilot project is often conducted in the organization's research and development (R&D) division under enriched conditions of highly educated, scientifically minded, and computer-experienced individuals.

One problem with pilot projects of such interactive media as electronic messaging systems is that a critical mass of users must be involved for it to provide a fair test of the new medium. If a user in the pilot project cannot contact another individual with the interactive system because that individual is not yet on the system, dissatisfaction and perhaps discontinuance will result. This problem of the critical mass is one reason a pilot project often involves all the individuals in an intact group like a company's R&D division or the households in a small community.

Expert judgment. One or more individuals who are especially knowledgeable about an interactive technology make their best intuitive estimate of the innovation's rate of adoption. Such a simple method of forecasting is sometimes more accurate than more statistical methods (Makridakis & Hibon, 1979).

Statistical prediction. Various statistical formulas can be used to predict the future rate of adoption of an innovation; usually these models predict later adoption from an innovation's early adoption. Bass (1969) developed the most widely used prediction model, which has been applied to forecasting the rate of adoption of cable television in the United States (Dodds, 1973) and VCR adoption in England (Lancaster & Wright, 1983). Unfortunately, these forecasts later proved to be inaccurate.

WHY ARE CERTAIN FORECASTING METHODS MORE ACCURATE?

Two common errors in technology assessment are *overestimating* the speed of diffusion of an innovation, and *underestimating* its eventual consequences and side effects. Pool (1983a, p. 1) concluded from his retrospective technology assessment of the telephone that "Market and technical analyses must be brought to bear simultaneously. Alone either of them fails; together they can produce some prescient forecasts." However, most technology assessments make little use of "market analysis"—that is, of the adoption or acceptability of the technological innovation.

Accuracy of a forecast is not always the most appropriate way to evaluate the quality of a forecast. For example, some forecasts may be accurate, but for the wrong reasons or strictly by coincidence (Klopfenstein, 1986). The evidence provided to support a forecast may be more important than just the accuracy of a forecast. Unfortunately, such evidence is seldom provided in forecasts of the new media's rate of adoption. For example, Klopfenstein (1986) identified twenty-nine forecasts of the future rate of adoption of home video (e.g., VCR or videodisc players). Little of the evidence used in making these forecasts was provided by the forecasters.

Forecasting the social impacts of a new communication technology is particularly hazardous because people do not necessarily use the new medium as originally intended or else it interacts with uses of other media. Frequently, the users find applications not previously contemplated. Adopters of home computers in the United States spend considerably less time watching television than do non-adopters (Dutton, Rogers & Jun, 1987)—a consequence completely unexpected by social forecasters. Similarly, computer use in the home reduces the average number of hours of sleep per night and the amount of time spend daily with other family members (Vitalari et al., 1985). Further, microcomputers were marketed for use in the home with the expectation that they would be used mainly in households with children for educational purposes, but the major actual use is for entertainment (videogames). Much work-related activity is done on home computers, such as word processing (Dutton, Rogers & Jun, 1987).

CAN 2 MILLION FRENCH PEOPLE BE WRONG?

By no means do all the expert forecasts for the new media far overshoot the reality that occurs. For example, the Minitel, a videotext service provided via telephone wires from the French PTT (Post, Telephone, and Telegraph), is a surprise of the other kind, with 1.8 million users in mid-1986, about 7 percent of all French telephone subscribers (Mayer, 1986). The Minitel system was launched in 1981 to compete with the United States and Japan in consumer electronics and to increase the volume of telephone use in France.

The Minitel provides a telephone directory of France's 34 million phone numbers, airline and train schedules, teleshopping, electronic messaging, and other information services. Initially, the terminal was free to French households. It cost about $165 to produce each Minitel (the price was low because the technology was kept simple—black-and-white, rather than color), and user fees, based on the type and amount of use, were added to monthly phone bills. The average household uses Minitel eighty-eight minutes per month, for about six calls, and pays about $12 per month (ten cents for forty-five seconds is a typical charge). As with many other new media, the distribution of use of Minitel is highly concentrated. Six percent of the 1.8 million users in France account for one third of the total use of the Minitel system (Mayer, 1986).

The French government originally expected that the main uses of

Minitel would be to obtain such information as train schedules, weather reports, and up-to-the-minute news plus use for telebanking and teleshopping. This forecast was wrong. Other than the electronic telephone directory service, the most popular Minitel service has been the interactive messaging centers (*messagerie*), which allow conversations between two or more people, usually anonymously. During the month of April 1986, the most popular *messagerie*, Le Parisien Libere, handled 1.7 million calls. The fifteen most-used *messageries* in France handled 6.6 million calls during that month. The most common topic of conversation was sex and dating; the French people use Minitel as the electronic equivalent of singles bars. In a country known for its love of talk and its talk of love, this romantic interactivity perhaps should not have come as a surprise to the engineers who designed the system. One important lesson to be derived from the Minitel experience is that a videotext system, though originally designed to provide information, will most likely be used for interactive interpersonal communication. Minitel was used like a telephone, not a newspaper (as had been forecast). French consumers appropriated this new medium and remolded it to suit unanticipated needs.

In the United States, where videotext was viewed by experts as a "publication" extension of the television set, several videotext systems (e.g., Knight-Ridder's Viewtron and Times-Mirror's Gateway) have been failures. In France, the government expects to make back its original investment, including the giveaway terminals, by 1989, eight years after an initial trial with 1,500 Minitel users.

Summary

An important research consideration with any medium is the adoption process. How do individuals or groups become aware of the new medium, decide to adopt it, or decide to stay with that adoption? Many early studies of the diffusions of innovations exist, but they differ somewhat from the new media, especially interactive media.

Any interactive medium has the special requirement of multiple adopters lest there be no individuals with whom to interact. This seems to impose an acceleration effect upon the traditional S-shaped curve that describes the rate of adoption. There is a "critical mass" at which there are sufficient users for adoption to "takeoff." Unlike many other studies of media, the nature of user interactions and how they may contribute to the critical mass concept is an important focus for new media research.

Research may seek insights into the adoption process, or forecast the rate or level of adoption. Forecasts do not have a reputation of being highly accurate.

Examples were given for ideal research, as well as studies of bulletin boards, electronic mail, and videotext media systems. In all, the quality of interactivity looms important. If ignored, forecasts of use may be especially erroneous.

The French videotext system, Minitel, is an example of the successful introduction of a new interactive medium; it is also a topic for new media research.

CHAPTER 6

Using Computer-Monitored Data

Automating Data Collection

A significant implication of the convergence of computers and tele-communication is that the new media can be used to collect comput-er-monitored data about how people use these media. "Computer-monitored data" is information collected automatically by a computer about the flow, type, content, or time of interaction by a person using the system. Such data are more common than one might expect. Consider the following three examples.

Data collected by the accounting software of information retrieval systems have been used to help design friendlier and more useful computer interfaces, to indicate which data-bases to develop, and to explore the processes by which users come to understand such systems.

Broadcasting executives, advertisers, and researchers use Nielsen or Arbitron ratings data collected automatically by devices attached to the television sets of a nationwide sample of U.S. television view-ers. These data measure how many television sets are tuned to partic-ular programs at quarter-hour intervals—the basic data for making television ratings. In 1986, a small keypad, called a people meter, was introduced in the United States (it had been first used by AGB, Inc., in Great Britain) to show which specific individuals in a household are viewing a particular television program, playing back a videocassette, or using the television set for viewing teletext. The keypad allows people in the house to enter their identification code whenever they watch television, and may be programmed to prompt the viewer to enter his or her code at regular time intervals. A small microprocessor installed in the television set collects information about which viewer is watching what program and conveys this information to the research company's main computer through a telephone line. Several marketing companies also provide respondents with a wandlike optical scanner that the respondents use to read the Universal Product Code (or bar code) on packages brought home from a shopping trip. This information is merged with the data collected by the people meter, allowing marketing researchers to match the respondents' television viewing of ads for certain products with their purchases of these products.

Personal computers provide new ways to collect data. Currently available software programs can measure usage by the account number of the user, by function, and by client or project (*PC Magazine*, 1986). Recently, surveys have been conducted by sending microcomputer diskettes through the mail with a cover letter asking individuals to respond interactively to question on the diskette. A computer merges and analyzes the data directly from the diskette after the respondent mails it back to the researcher. This computer-monitored process reduces errors and time otherwise involved in rekeying the data into a computer file (Chase Manhattan Bank, for example, in 1987 mailed survey diskettes to 2,500 business executives who use personal computers). The diskette software also allows respondents to try out free sample software using their own data. The same computer that enables individuals to use electronic messaging systems to process and share messages, documents, data, and co-authored articles with others has been used to collect data about the content and patterns of this new form of interactive communication.

In this chapter we discuss the characteristics and research uses of computer-monitored data.

Characteristics of Computer-Monitored Data

ADVANTAGES FOR VALIDITY AND RELIABILITY

Computer-monitored data have certain advantages with respect to several types of threats to the validity and reliability of research. One threat to the internal validity of a study is that the data may have been collected in an obtrusive or reactive way, in which the process of collecting the data may have affected the respondents' answers or the sample (Webb et al., 1966; see also Chapter 4). Computer-monitored data reduce the obtrusiveness of data collection. One threat to the reliability of a study is a possible bias in the ways that the data are measured or reported. Computer-monitored data, therefore, are typically reliable measures of what they purport to measure. One threat to the external validity of a study is that self-report measures often are inadequate or biased measures of usage of a system or of the other individuals with whom the respondent communicates. Computer-monitored data are usually different from data collected by questionnaires or case studies, so they are an important component of triangulation (Chapter 3). (Chapter 12 discusses issues of privacy and ethics in collecting and analyzing such computer-monitored data.)

COMPARING COMPUTER-MONITORED DATA TO SELF-REPORT DATA

Computer communication systems collect data that are accurate and reliable records of communication behavior on the computer system. These characteristics are especially important because past research shows that individuals' attitudes are only moderately correlated with their behavior (Berger & Roloff, 1980). Also, respondents' reports of a wide range of behaviors may be biased and divergent from their behavior (Bernard et al., 1984). And different methods of collecting communication data (such as diaries, observations, and questionnaires) result in over- or underestimations of communication behavior (Hartley et al., 1977).

Eskin (1985) collected Nielsen measures of exposure to cable television programs advertising a certain product, people meter data on consumption of the product by viewers of the programs, and self-reported consumption of the product (and viewing of the program) through a survey. These data showed that 86 percent of the sample reported buying the product, although only 64 percent had actually bought it. Further, television viewers were much more likely to switch channels during a commercial shown in the middle of a program than between programs. And the viewing of commercials about a product was related to increased purchases of that product at local stores by the respondents.

Computer-monitored measures of individuals' use of a communication system are typically only moderately correlated (about 16 to 36 percent of common variance) with self-reported measures of these individuals' use of the new medium. However, self-reports are not necessarily inaccurate, and computer-monitored measures are not always the most valid indicators of system use. The two measures may represent conceptually different aspects of human communication. A self-report measure may operationalize a generalized "average" degree of use rather than the detailed numbers of messages or time spent using a communication system. Further, computer-monitored data cannot indicate the prior social realities, importance, meaning, or redundancy of the uses of a communication system. User perceptions can best be ascertained by personal interviews. As a result of these and other differences, the two types of measures can play different roles in the analysis of a communication system.

Indeed, research is beginning to reveal how these measures differ. Sociodemographic and information-seeking variables tend to be differentially associated with computer-monitored usage versus self-reported usage. The two forms of usage data appear differentially associated with the benefits that respondents perceive from using a computer-communication system (Ettema, 1985). Further, computerized, voluntary questionnaires tend to have similar response rates but a higher degree of variance in the responses than written questionnaires (Kiesler & Sproull, 1986; Sproull, 1986). Voluntary paper questionnaires and voluntary on-line surveys are often answered by slightly different kinds of respondents (Newsted, 1985).

Although computer-monitored data may be more reliable, less obtrusive, and have inherently less measurement error than self-report data, they are not the only valid or sufficient measures of system use. The differences between computer-monitored and self-report data discussed here are a strong argument for a triangulation strategy in studying the new media (Chapter 3).

Research Uses of Computer-Monitored Data

MONITORING AND INITIATING

Procedures for collecting computer-monitored data can take either an unobtrusive, monitoring form *or* a more obtrusive, initiating form.

The computer system as monitor. A computer communication system can collect data unobtrusively—that is, data may be collected as part of the computer system's own rcord-keeping, without any particular action required from the user. System data may be archival—

that is, collected historically by the system, stored at some time in the past, and retrieved later, perhaps even after the individuals are no longer using the system. System data may also be "real-time," whereby automatic reports of system usage can be collected and analyzed on a daily, weekly, or monthly basis. Although the collection of data is transparent, informed consent agreements signed by the users to allow such data-collection, and other reasons why individuals might be aware of this monitoring, may make the study quite obtrusive. Such awareness might in turn change how people use—or do not use—the interactive communication system.

The computer system as initiator. Computer communication systems can also be designed to be obtrusive initiators of communication behavior. The computer can be programmed to:

- Structure group communication
- Deliver timed messages and collect responses in on-line controlled experiments
- Randomly assign treatments to individuals in experiments
- Replicate instructions and measures
- Remind or enable users to provide data
- Determine the duration and timing of communication events
- Collect data in on-line surveys

Types of Data and Research Design Elements

Computer-monitored data can be used to measure a variety of communication behaviors and to assist in achieving appropriate research designs. We summarize five categories here.

1. *Usage.* The degree to which an individual uses a computer communication system can be shown by the amount of time spent using the system (duration), the number of log-ons to the system (frequency), the amount of time since the user first logged on to the system (exposure), the kinds of commands used, or the type and number of computer files that are accessed. These different operationalizations measure conceptually different aspects of use (Chapter 4).

2. *Networks.* The communication structure of a system can be indicated by the patterns of messages exchanged among its users

(Chapter 11). Most communication network studies rely on questionnaires or personal interviews to measure who communicates with
whom. Such data-gathering methods are limited to a moderately
sized network to avoid unreasonable demands on respondents, are
subject to missing responses, and are susceptible to biases in respondents' self-reports of network contacts (even in response to questions about who they sent messages to, or received messages from,
within the last hour). In contrast, network studies that analyze computer-monitored data are less limited by the capabilities of network
analysis programs, the memory constraints of the computer, and the
accuracy of computer records. But the programming required to process the who-to-whom data into a usable format may be considerable.
Further, just like observational or survey network data, computer-
monitored network data must be interpreted in light of the context
and structure of the ongoing communication system of study. For
example, international standards and telecommunications policies
may enable researchers working on the same project to keep in touch
via a conferencing system.

3. *Sampling.* Researchers can use computer communication systems to collect a full census of communication behaviors, users, time
frames, sets of commands, linkages among users, computer features
used, and content. Several of the possible weaknesses of surveys,
such as nonprobability samples, missing responses, and high
variance due to small sample size, can be avoided by using a census.
External validity may be weakened, though, because it may be difficult to generalize to users of other systems or to nonusers. Unique
problems can occur with computer-mediated data-collection. For instance, consider an on-line questionnaire sent to the computer accounts on a list provided by an organization, a community association,
or a computer users' group. The researcher should check to determine if any of these computer accounts are used by multiple individuals, by the same individual, or represent "distribution lists" of
another set of individual accounts.

4. *Content.* The complete text or just the headers of messages
exchanged via a computer communication system can be analyzed for
their content, interaction episodes, and the co-occurrence of words or
phrases (Danowski, 1987). Capturing the text directly avoids the
lengthy and error-prone process of transcribing conversations, allows
a researcher to compare several analytical strategies, and enables two
or more researchers to share textual content much more easily. Computer-based content analysis was developed in the mid-1960s by Phil-

ip Stone of Harvard University in his General Inquirer computer program (Stone & Dunphy, 1966). This early approach typically required retyping of a text into a computer. Today, the content can be entered directly into a computer communication medium. For example, a newspaper wire service allows researchers to content analyze large on-line data-bases of news stories.

5. *Process.* A computer can be programmed to collect the messaging or command activities of users whenever they log on and do this without questionnaires, personal interviews, diaries, or other explicitly obtrusive data-gathering techniques. It is far easier to collect longitudinal communication data by computer than by more obtrusive means. These data may be continuous, such as all the messages exchanged among a network of users, including the exact time each message was sent or received, or discrete, representing summary statistics for specific time periods. Such extensive data-sets allow researchers to study how users develop patterns of interaction over time, how themes in computer conference comments develop and eventually disappear, and how group members interact with different other individuals as a network matures over time.

AN EXAMPLE SHOWING A COMBINATION OF USES

The following example illustrates how each of these forms of computer-monitored data can be combined in one analysis. Rice and Love (1987) analyzed the content and network relationships in six weeks of transcripts from a U.S. public computer bulletin board SIG (special interest group) used by medical doctors and nurses. Computer communication systems are often assumed to hinder communication of a more personal and emotional nature because of the limited ability of computer-based text to transmit all the social and nonverbal cues of face-to-face communication. However, 30 percent of the message content on the computer bulletin board was of a personal or social nature. There was no significant difference between the percentage of messages of social content sent within network groups and that sent across network groups. The degree of social content was not a basis for the patterns of computer communication. A person's propensity for social communication on the computer bulletin board did not change over time. Table 6–1 provides an example of the content, relational identification, and coding categories for one message from this computer bulletin board.

Table 6-1. A Simple Message from Compuserve's Medsig
Public Computer Bulletin Board

#:	13232	Sec. 0-GENERAL/MISC
Sb:	#13207-NURSING	
	10-Feb-84	23:52:51
Fm:	(Node 54)	
To:	(Node 8)	

Speaking of nursing, how many nurses are there who participate in this SIG? My girlfriend is a nurse, and I am trying to nurture an interest in computers.

Note: The users' names and account numbers have been replaced by an identification code. Based upon the coding scheme for group processes and communication context developed by Bales (1950), the first sentence was coded as "Asks for information—professional" (task-related content) and the second was coded as "Gives information—personal" (social content).

RETESTING THE ERIE COUNTY STUDY WITH COMPUTER-MONITORED SURVEYS

The following on-line survey example illustrates the use of a computer system to initiate both quantitative responses and qualitative open-ended content from a random sample of respondents over time. The results challenge established findings from an earlier survey. Perhaps one of the most influential political communication research projects is the Erie County study of the 1940 presidential election (Lazarsfeld et al., 1944). This investigation cast an important shadow over later research and theory because it concluded that the mass media were surprisingly unimportant in how voters decided between the Democratic and Republican presidential candidates. This finding led the researchers to, first, make the general claim that mass media communication had only minimal effects and, then, to propose a two-step flow of communication in which opinion leaders are influenced by the media and in turn influence their followers by interpersonal communication.

The researchers thought they had designed the perfect study to measure media effects. A sample of 600 respondents in Erie County, Ohio, was asked about their voting intentions at six monthly intervals prior to the November election. Whenever a respondent's voting intention changed from the previous month, an attempt was made to ascertain whether the mass media or interpersonal communication was responsible for the change. However, only 54 of the 600 respondents reported ever changing their minds. Based on this low level of change, the researchers decided that mass media had little effect on voters' decisions.

Seth Finn (1987), a professor of mass communication at the University of North Carolina (UNC), decided to use a computerized survey system to measure voting changes in the 1984 North Carolina general election. In this system, the Computer Administered Panel Study (CAPS), a random sample of nearly a hundred UNC undergraduates was interviewed by a computer for an hour and a half at twenty weekly intervals during a semester. Table 6–2 lists advantages of on-line polling using CAPS.

Finn gathered data from his panel in five waves; on each occasion the CAPS asked his respondents how they intended to vote for president, senator, and governor using a seven-point scale (this measure was more sensitive than the Lazarsfeld et al. measure of voting choice between Roosevelt or Wilkie as a dichotomous variable). The CAPS compared each student respondent's voting preferences from the previous wave (which was stored by CAPS) with his or her most recent preferences to determine if a change had occurred. If so, CAPS recorded verbatim responses to open-ended questions about what information led to the voting shift and the channel through which this information was conveyed.

There were ninety-one shifts (of at least one category on the seven-point voting intention scale) across the three election races for the eighty-seven respondents, but only seventy-five could be classi-

Table 6–2. Advantages of On-line Surveys

1. A permanent panel of participants is available each semester, with low (8 percent) attrition.
2. The turnaround of results is quick.
3. Longitudinal data-analysis is possible.
4. Cost of data-collection is minimal.
5. Modules of questions, including open-ended items, can be added and revised quickly.
6. Participants get immediate, on-line feedback.
7. Data entry is checked for errors in real time.
8. Data are automatically analyzed.
9. Data are automatically archived.
10. Teams or groups of respondents can participate.
11. Experiments can be administered.
12. Other researchers can compare and cross-analyze the data.

SOURCE: Adapted from Hiltz (1979) and Latane (1987).

fied as to their primary source of information. Only fifteen shifts were attributed to interpersonal channels, while twenty-nine were attributed to radio/television broadcasts and twenty-three to print. Opinion leaders apparently translated the print information into oral forms for easier processing by their followers, but this function was handled by television in major elections. Despite the small sample, the UNC findings strongly contradict those of Lazarsfeld et al. (1944).

Merging Computer-Monitored Data with Questionnaire Data

DATA COMBINATIONS

Computer-monitored data can be combined with self-reported survey data as the following study by Rice and Shook (1988) shows. The process is often lengthy and complex, but it can be rewarding. The study concerned the use of an integrated office system known as PROFS (Professional Office System, a trademark of the International Business Machines Corporation). PROFS operates on an organization's mainframe computer and provides a wide range of office functions, such as electronic messaging, document filing and retrieval, appointment calendars, graphics, editorial and style modules for document preparation, and basic calculations. The research site was a high-technology division of a *Fortune* 1,000 aerospace company.

Sources of data for the study included: (1) a questionnaire administered to 133 PROFS account holders one year after the system was implemented; (2) usage of the system by all account holders, collected by the mainframe's accounting system; and (3) personal interviews with PROFS users. The computer system's documentation indicated that the computer stored a variety of information, as shown in Table 6–3, at the end of every user's session.

PROBLEMS

Several problems arose in trying to merge the computer-monitored and self-report data-sets.

The computer system did not capture usage data according to a fixed weekly or monthly schedule, but according to the computer's processing schedule and memory capacity. Therefore, the organiza-

Table 6–3. Description of Measures Collected by *PROFS* as Listed in the Software Documentation Manual

Column	Contents	Format
1–8	Identification (ID) of the user	character
. . .		. . .
17–28	Data and time of use (mmddyyhhmmss) (month, day, year, hour, minute, second)	numeric
29–32	Number of seconds connected to the computer	hexadecimal
. . .		. . .
. . .		. . .
79–80	End of record	numeric

tion provided twenty separate files, representing time periods ranging from a few days to a month, on two computer tapes.

Because the computer captured so much other data (columns 33 through 78) for all the users of the system, the data files were too large to be stored on most computer systems or be handled by most computer data-analysis systems. The total storage size of the second tape was sixty megabytes. Therefore, the researchers planned to read and store only a few desired variables into a statistical computer package directly from the two tapes.

Unfortunately, the organization's accounting system and the researchers' accounts and statistical programs ran on different operating systems, so the files could not be read directly from the organization's computer tapes. Although special programs (a "utility") to convert data from one system to another are available, neither the organization nor the university had a copy. In the end, a student consultant worked after hours to transfer the data through a third system.

Although the documentation indicated that the format for the date and time was "mmddyyhhmmss" (month, day, year, hour, minute, second), the computer program that read these data showed "format errors." Inspecting some sample records in raw form revealed that the format actually was "yymmddhhmmss." The documentation also indicated that the data in columns 29 to 80 were in *hexadecimal* format (a way the computer stores data in compressed form). By again inspecting sample records (using the "alternate format viewing facility" of the computer's operating system), it became clear that the connect time measure was actually in *integer binary* format (another way the computer can store compressed data). Fortunately, the statistical data-analysis package could read data in either of these formats and convert it to a usable one.

What are the basic lessons here? Look carefully at the raw form of your data. Question the formal documentation of the computer software program when you receive errors during input of raw data. And try to find help for unique problems that are certain to arise.

MERGING THE DATA

Once the data were properly read in to the statistical package, and the twenty separate time-period data files were backed up on tape, each period was prepared for processing. The Statistical Analysis System (SAS) was used to read the files, combine them, calculate summary variables for all the users, and merge these data with the self-report survey data.

Other problems arose that were common to most studies that merge computer-monitored data with self-report data, such as identifying those individuals who had answered a questionnaire but did not have a computer account and those who had a computer account but did not answer a questionnaire. Other situations include users with several computer accounts, misrecording of user identification numbers on the organization's roster, several users who share a single computer account, and accounts that have been reassigned from an initial user (who may have left the organization) to a later new user. These tasks were done by using the statistical package to merge or match the questionnaire data with the computer-monitored data, to identify the cases that have missing values for all the questionnaire variables or the usage data, and then to delete those cases and create a new file.

Figure 6-1 portrays, in simplified form, how the computer-monitored data measuring PROFS usage over time by the sample of respondents was combined with cross-sectional questionnaire data collected from those respondents at one point in time. Because the system collected the date that the user first logged on to the system, the program for merging the data could also calculate the number of weeks since that first log-on. For example, Figure 6-1 shows that questionnaire respondent #2 first logged on about twelve weeks before the questionnaire was administered. Questionnaire respondent #8 never logged on to PROFS, so there is no computer-monitored data; the value for exposure therefore is zero. The analysis could

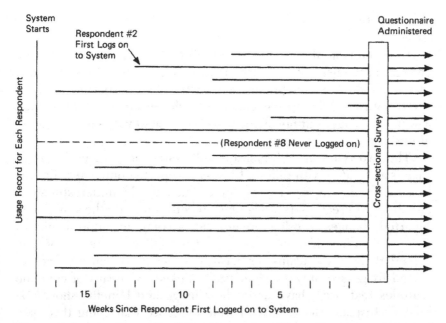

Figure 6–1. An Example of Combining Over-Time Computer-Monitored Usage Records with Cross-Sectional Survey Data Collected by Questionnaire

include the influence of exposure to PROFS, as well as the influence of levels of frequency and duration of system use, on attitudes and behaviors reported on the questionnaire.

RESULTS

To give an idea of the relative values of the different measures of usage, the average number of log-ons per day was 1.9, and the average number of computer-monitored minutes of use per day was 57.8. The average number of self-reported minutes per day was 27.9. Thus, the amount of time per day as measured by the computer system was about twice what the respondents reported—a considerable discrepancy.

The merged file allowed us to compute correlations among self-reported and computer-monitored data. Computer-monitored minutes of use per day were strongly correlated ($r = .60$) with self-reported minutes per day using PROFS. Although the correlation is significantly different from zero, only 36 percent of the variance is shared between measures of computer-monitored and self-reported usage.

Computer-monitored usage of PROFS was correlated with changes in the use of traditional organizational communication media (personal contacts, telephone, and letters). Self-reported usage of PROFS was slightly less correlated with changes in personal contacts and phone usage, but not significantly correlated with changes in use of letters.

The two types of data measure different aspects of usage. Also, each is associated with different levels of reported outcomes. Results based only on the self-report survey data would underestimate—although not greatly—the relationship between using the system and reported changes in other organizational communication activities. Using only the self-report data would not allow the researchers to defend their study against criticism that reported benefits and reported usage are only psychologically linked by means of common attitudes that users have about how usage and benefits should be related. Instead, the results provide evidence that using this electronic messaging system led to predictable, if small, changes in organizational communication.

Summary

The use of computer-monitored data is one step toward improving the infrastructure of communication research (Latane, 1987). Such data provide greater access to large data-sets of longitudinal, archival (perhaps unobtrusive), and reliable measures of communication linkages and content, often at lower expense than alternative methods of data-gathering. The present chapter summarized studies that used computer-monitored data in fruitful ways to extend theories, methods, and understanding of human use and interpretation of the new media.

Many new issues are raised by the availability of such data.

How strong is the internal as well as external validity of computer-monitored content and network data, which may not reflect the meanings and social realities of the participants in a communication system?

How strong is the construct validity of computer-monitored measures compared to self-report measures? If they are only moderately correlated with each other, and are associated differently with other variables, is either type of measure more valid than the other?

Is it acceptable and proper to collect computer-monitored data from users regardless of the extent to which standard guarantees of confidentiality are provided? (See Chapter 12.)

The availability of such new data requires new skills and expertise for research. Will researchers have sufficient training in the programming and data-management that are required to handle computer-monitored data?

Thus, computer-monitored communication data provide opportunities and challenges, advantages and disadvantages to communication researchers studying the new media.

Note

The authors would like to acknowledge Douglas Shook for his helpful advice on computer programming discussed in this chapter.

CHAPTER 7

Strategies for Studying Cases

Why Do a Case Study?

In 1982, a major topic of discussion at summer meetings of school administrators in the Los Angeles area was a growing concern over the increasing number of microcomputers finding their way into the public schools. "Finding their way" was an appropriate description because, unlike usual changes in school curriculum or equipment, there had been no systematic plan underlying the acquisition of these computers.

During that same summer, a project was in the early stages of development at the Annenberg School of Communications at the University of Southern California to study the implementation of microcomputers in typical public school settings (Williams & Williams, 1984). Initially, the researchers had intended to conduct a survey, and their first contact with Los Angeles County school officials was to request cooperation in developing the questionnaire. The school officials, however, reported that a survey had recently been undertaken, and its results were of little value because computers were arriving in the schools faster than it was possible to develop a suitable questionnaire, distribute it, and carefully analyze the results.

Insight was needed into how schools intended to implement microcomputers, information that would be useful not only for school district coordination, but for schools to learn from each other. Studying fewer schools in depth, particularly with a qualitative emphasis, could yield much more useful information than a widely distributed quantitative survey. So a case study approach was adopted. On the plus side was that more detailed scenarios of experiences with micro-computer implementation would be developed and shared among schools and with the district. On the negative side was that the research would be more subjective and less rigorously representative than a survey.

In this chapter, we examine some of the reasons for conducting case studies, especially where new media are involved. There are case studies of communication media not only in many different educational settings, but in the home, the office, and health care environments, to name a few. We will also describe more details of the microcomputer implementation study that serves as our introductory example.

Another potential dividend of the case study approach is that "cases," such as the Harvard Business School case studies, also provide an excellent basis for learning and teaching. The management of communication media can benefit from insights into well-researched cases.

What Defines a Case Study?

Wilbur Schramm (n.d., p. 1), a pioneer in instructional media research, once characterized the case study approach as one that "organizes the details of life in search of patterns and insights." In less succinct terms, a case study is a descriptive type of research undertaking in which individuals, groups, or organizations are interviewed or observed, or various types of archival records are examined. The case approach may use less formally structured methods at the outset than a typical survey or experiment. This is not to imply that case studies are by their nature unplanned; it is that there is more flexibility than in most other observational research methods. Also, the case study may often be more qualitative in approach, or may freely mix quantitative and qualitative approaches, or seek a triangulation of findings (Chapter 3).

Robert K. Yin, in his book *Case Study Research* (1984, p. 13), holds that case studies are valuable when the phenomena under study are contemporary and not under the control of the researcher, yet there is a desire to answer "how" or "when" questions. He argues against the presumption held by some that case studies are a weak "stepsister" of other research methods. He sees them as valuable for research into community or organizational behaviors, or policy, political science, and public administration research. All such applications are most relevant to communication media studies where we are interested in the adoption of an innovation, regulatory policy, or administrative issues. Yin's definition (p. 23) of the case study is that of an empirical inquiry that:

- Investigates a contemporary phenomenon with its real-life context; when
- The boundaries between phenomenon and context are not clearly evident; and in which
- Multiple sources of evidence are used.

Sometimes case studies are valuable in applying a mix of observational methods to compare results or interpretations—that is, to attempt triangulation (Webb et al., 1966).

A major shortcoming of case studies is the inability to test cause-and-effect relationships because some type of experimental control, including a suitable control group, is not involved. The settings for case studies are organized primarily for accomplishment of some operational objective rather than as an object for research. At best, the case study researcher tries to superimpose data-gathering that will capture a description of the key phenomena and not interfere with the main operational objectives. However, the case study has the important advantage of allowing us to study a process over time, sometimes a key problem for research. Finally, there is the challenge of aggregating data from case studies into higher level generalizations. Unlike the statistical methods available for developing generalizations from quantitative, or even semiquantified qualitative, data, case studies offer few standard methods for reasoning from the particular contexts to generalizations about other contexts.

On the other hand, case studies can yield valuable results; otherwise they would not be employed so frequently. The present example of the microcomputer implementation case study in Los Angeles represents a typical situation where a case study is applicable. Qualitative, in-depth information was gathered from a few representative cases to gain a sense of the "what" and "how" aspects of the situation. Quantitative information from a random sample of schools was not needed for making the decisions at hand. The most useful information was readily interpretable in human terms—namely, what individuals in different schools were doing with microcomputers and why they took their courses of action.

Case studies are particularly valuable when:

- Qualitative, descriptive information is needed to introduce the investigator to a new research situation.
- There is no particular need for a random sample of respondents as a basis for generalization of the research results to a larger population.
- "Sagas" or "scenarios" may be a preferred or useful level of data generalization, especially if they describe a process over time.
- A study has to be conducted rapidly while there is the opportunity.
- There is a need to do preliminary fact-finding in an area to be later researched with more rigorous methods.

Again, many of these qualities make case studies a valuable approach for studying communication media. For one thing, the technologies are often changing, not only in themselves but in how they are being used. As in the microcomputer example in this chapter, there may not be time to wait for a settling-in period. It is the process of implementation that is of interest to us. On the negative side are the following:

Do not usually expect the following from case studies:

- Test of cause-effect models
- Generalizing to a population from a random sample of cases
- Tests of hypotheses (possible under some circumstances)
- Use of inferential statistical methods
- A high degree of objectivity
- Acceptance as valuable research when more suitable research methods could have been reasonably applied

Microcomputers in the Schools: A Case Study Example

BACKGROUND AND PROBLEM

According to one district administrator in Los Angeles, the arrival of microcomputers was a hodgepodge. In one school, the PTA raised money to buy two dozen computers from a local electronics discount store. In another school, a wealthy patron funded a fully equipped laboratory, the only demand being that the machines be bought and installed within one week's time. In another example, the school board mandated that their district begin instruction in "computer literacy" (which has a wide variety of definitions) and that the laboratory must include examples of at least five major brands of computers. In another school, children from a wealthy neighborhood were encouraged to bring their computers to school to engage in what was anticipated as "computer-assisted instruction."

Under such conditions, it was impossible for the schools to benefit from shared software or common computer textbook selections. The primary challenge for research at the time was simply to know what each of the different schools was doing with microcomputers. As mentioned in the introduction to this chapter, these were the reasons for using a case study approach. We wanted to identify outstanding ideas for implementation so that the district office could document and promote their wider use. Further, the district could follow up with suggested curriculum, textbook, and teacher-training programs.

The research program was framed by three general questions:

1. What is the status of computer implementation in these schools?
2. What types of implementation activities can be developed?
3. What implications can schools share with one another for effective implementation of microcomputers?

METHOD

With the help of the school district office and several other organizations, fifteen schools from the Southern California area were selected for study (most were from Los Angeles County, with several from Ventura and Orange counties). These schools were selected not because of any extraordinary use of, or plans for, computers. It was mainly because they represented "ordinary" types of schools in the system, where experiences with computers could likely be valuable to other schools of their general type. Accordingly, these schools, all of them at the elementary level, were distinguished primarily by their locations: central city, suburban, or semirural. Of the fifteen schools selected for the study, twelve were eventually studied in detail. One school withdrew and two others did not receive the expected microcomputers by the time of the study.

Data gathering about the status of computer implementation (question #1 above) focused on the brands and models of computers acquired, cost, source of funds, individuals in charge of acquisition, likely uses of the computers, and information on the schools themselves (number of students, budget, etc.). This was more or less an "inventory" type of operation. Data for implementation scenarios (question #2) were gathered as responses to open-ended questions posed to administrators, teachers, and some students. What was their perception of how computers had "arrived" in the school? Who was in charge? What were the overall objectives and the timetable for implementing them? What were the major successes and failures? What advice would the implementors give to other schools? What support activities or material did they especially seek from the district? How would they do the implementation if they had a second chance? These questions were used in personal interviews by individual members of the research team who were assigned to respective schools. The answers to question #3 on sharing information came partly from asking questions on this in the interviews, but mainly in the researchers' interpretation of what information would be valuable to other schools.

The research staff made successive visits to the schools over about a one-month period. During that time, the research team met twice per week to discuss their observations in the different schools and to assist one another in suggesting further types of observations, interpretations, and to see contrasts among the different schools. Members of the research team were also instructed to attempt to write a "scenario" of the implementation process in their particular schools.

The data from the schools, including the scenarios, were compiled into the central computer files where the directors of the research could compare results and begin to write overall generalizations. The twice-weekly discussion sessions allowed the researchers to check one anothers' biases. One example of bias was where a scenario might initially concentrate on uses of computers in math classes because that teacher offered more information in the interviews than did, say, a language arts teacher. In later visits to the school, the researcher might then intentionally seek out other examples of computer use. In each of the schools, attempts were made to discuss implementation with not only teachers and administrators, but as much as was possible with parents and pupils.

RESULTS

A draft report of the results was distributed to the research team, to various officials in the county school district office, and to at least one individual in each of the twelve schools that were studied. All these individuals were then contacted for comment or corrections to the draft report.

Although basic data gathered on equipment and software were of value to the school district, what eventually became most useful were the implementation scenarios of the different schools. These scenarios provided the schools with many ideas for successful implementation. For example, there were often questions about how to gain funds for the purchase of software. That some schools allocated a percentage of textbook funds for this purpose was often welcome as an idea or a precedent. There was also considerable interest in methods for preevaluation of software, type of forms to use, sources of reviews, or sample materials. Several of the schools in the study suggested that additional valuable information be added as appendixes to the project report. These included a glossary of microcomputing terms, a directory of courseware manufacturers, and an annotated bibliography of research and popular articles on microcomputer implementation in schools. Some of the different scenarios can be seen from the titles of selected chapters in the project report and in a later book (Williams & Williams, 1984):

> Exploring with Computers
> The Principal Is the Innovator
> District Plan for Implementation
> Creating a Computer Lab
> One Teacher Takes the Lead
> Computers in a Magnet School
> A Computer-Scientist Parent Implements
> A Private School Adopts Computers
> Teaching How to Think
> Computers for Gifted Students
> Computers for Remedial Instruction
> Parents Meet the Challenge

One major need voiced by individuals in most of the schools studied was for help in software (or "courseware") acquisition. For many of the schools, the lesson of first-time implementation was that computers were of little value without appropriate programs, and these were not all that readily available. This need became a major priority for help from the district, leading to its definition as the topic of a follow-up study (Williams & Williams, 1985).

General Steps for Designing a Case Study

1. Specify the Need for a Case Study

Your first question should be whether there is a need for case study research. Is your research a "first step" in investigating a new problem area? Are qualitative descriptions desired? Can you forgo random sampling? Moreover, remember that a definite advantage of a case study is that the research activities can be modified as the study progresses. During the course of the Los Angeles microcomputer study, the values of the scenarios became increasingly evident, and they were emphasized more in later interviews and observations. Also, as consensus developed about the problems of software acquisition, practices in this area were studied in more detail. In all, especially in a rapidly developing area, it is difficult to anticipate all the details necessary for a one-time questionnaire construction or an experimental design. At the risk of subjectivity, case studies offer flexibility to adapt to a changing situation.

Initial research planning requires a specific statement of the research problem, which for a case study is usually a statement of objectives or, better, a set of specific questions to be answered. Given this statement, be sure that your research activities will focus on specific answers. Anticipate that the results section of your research report will be organized point by point or question by question in terms of your problem statement.

2. Define the Unit of Analysis

In research design terms, you must decide what will constitute the basic unit of study or the "case." It might be individuals, groups, or organizations, or even some type of process or behavior identified across a variety of contexts. Although you will not usually use formal sampling methods, your cases should subjectively represent some larger universe of cases. Although the process of microcomputer implementation was the focus for the above described study, we considered the different schools as units for analysis, or as the "cases," and we had a rationale (described earlier) for selecting them. Among the practical reasons for defining a particular unit for analysis is that a similar definition is used in previous research literature (so results can be compared), or the unit is a common focus in whatever phenomenon is being studied (so you can communicate about it).

A case study design might include an overall pattern of research into individual cases structured to lead to cross-case generalizations. Yin (1984, p. 51) illustrates this approach particularly well in the diagram shown in Figure 7–1. Note how the process can accumulate evidence across a series of individual cases. In brief, carefully identify the criteria used in selecting your cases for study, consider how they may be related to cross-case comparisons, then, as a part of your research plan, specify the case or cases to be researched.

3. PLAN DATA-GATHERING AND ANALYSES

There are many alternatives for gathering case study data, including the opportunity to gather different types of data, especially as they serve as "checks" on one another. There may be questionnaires for gathering specific information, but open-ended questions will offer

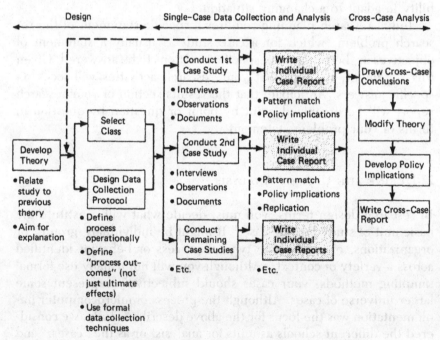

Figure 7–1. Case Study Method Involving Multiple Cases

SOURCE: R. K. Yin, *Case Study Research*, p. 51. Copyright © 1984 by Sage Publications, Inc. Reprinted by permission of Sage Publications, Inc.

opportunity for exploring selected topics in depth. Observations can be recorded as well as data gathered from existing records. Respondents might be asked to fill in reports, to write scenarios, or to describe their evaluation of a situation. Remember, too, to maintain some flexibility so that data-gathering can be modified or augmented as the research progresses. Rechecking certain key types of data will add to objectivity. Prior research into cases of a similar nature to those under study will often be the best guide for data-gathering procedures.

As mentioned earlier, case studies can often benefit from triangulation of methods for studying the same phenomenon. In the microcomputer study, some triangulation occurred in comparing our "inventory" type results with the narratives of individuals in describing computer implementation. The study might well have included studies of cost records to cross-check other results.

Do not go into the field without your data-gathering instruments in order and your researchers trained to use them. Be certain that data are reported in standard formats that can be easily accessed, reviewed, and summarized. For instance, note that in the Los Angeles case study, we gathered quantitative data (e.g., numbers of machines) in each school as well as the more qualitative scenarios of microcomputer implementation.

4. CARRY OUT THE RESEARCH PLAN

As in the present example, case studies are best undertaken by a research team, which may lessen the bias imposed by a single individual. Yet having a research team requires the ability of members to communicate effectively with one another and to derive consensus both on what has been observed and the generalizations drawn from those observations. Be sure to gather data on a definite schedule. This is important not only to expedite the study but to ensure that cases are studied in a similar time frame.

Anticipate the analyses and final report of your research as data are gathered. Interim analyses give you an early glimpse of likely results and provide a basis for checking results with respondents or making ongoing adjustments in the research design. As in our Los Angeles study, have a strategy—for example, a common computer file—for developing the report as the study progresses.

Finally, having third-party researchers—individuals from the case studies, consultants, or other experts—review the preliminary data often leads to study refinements and facilitates objectivity. The principles of interpretive research (Chapter 3) require that case studies be written in language meaningful and interpretable by the participants. Participants should have the opportunity to comment on, and share in, the interim results. Further, case studies should provide ongoing insights that require revision or re-examination of interim results.

Summary

Case studies are especially valuable when studying the new media because many applications of new technologies are constantly changing. Despite the somewhat less formal methods used in studying cases, the approach is valuable for answering "how" or "when" questions. One should not feel that the case study is a "lesser" method than other approaches; it is often more appropriate. Also, case studies can be enhanced by triangulation approaches.

An example of a case study of the introduction of microcomputers in Los Angeles County schools illustrated the approach and advantages of this method in studying a new media system.

Steps for designing a case study include: (1) specify the need, (2) define the unit of analysis, (3) plan data-gathering and analyses, and (4) carry out the research plan.

CHAPTER 8

Implementing Formative Evaluation

A "Developmental" Approach

As the name implies, "formative" evaluation refers to research that is done during the development or formative stage of media or product development. This research is in contrast to "summative" evaluation, or research that assesses a final product and summarizes the results of a completed study. The chief purpose of formative evaluation is to improve the product or service while it is being developed, by giving feedback to the developers. Although formative types of evaluation are reflected in a wide variety of developmental activities, including market research, it is best known in communication studies as applied to the assessment of educational media materials. Perhaps the best-known application of formative evaluation was its key role in the development of "Sesame Street" (Palmer, 1974) as well as other programs of the Children's Television Workshop. Michael Scriven (1980) has also written extensively on the application of formative evaluation to educational research. Recently, formative evaluation has been analyzed with respect to computer communication systems (Rice, 1988).

Formative studies may range from a series of informal evaluations, often *ad hoc* in nature, to a formal plan for evaluation at selected stages of a project. Often, formative evaluation is applied in the development of program materials. For example, in Chapter 11 we describe a study of how an interactive videodisc changed the behavior of cancer patients and their relatives regarding hair loss due to radiation treatment of cancer (Van Tassel, 1987). About six months were required to gather data about behavior changes resulting from using the videodisc from a sample of fifty-four immediate others of cancer patients. But more than three years was needed to design and create the videodisc program and to complete formative evaluation research to ensure that the software program accurately and effectively conveyed the intended information about hair loss. The interactive nature of the videodisc, while providing important advantages for effective communication about this sensitive topic, posed important problems for the formative evaluation process.

The adoption of new communication media places a special emphasis on the "implementation" process—that is, all the events, persons, and circumstances surrounding the adoption of a new idea. No new media program or technology can be effective without a successful implementation sequence, and the more we know about that sequence the better we can plan it. Until implementation has occurred, the innovation process remains a mental exercise. Johnson and Rice's (1987) study of the implementation of word processing in office environments, although not in itself formative research, reflects on the importance of the implementation process that could be researched in a formative context.

Very often, serious problems occur when one attempts to implement a new technology, especially when the adopting unit is an organization rather than an individual. In an organization, many individuals are usually involved in implementation, and the implementors are often a different set of people from those who planned the innovation, and both are different from the individuals who are most affected by the innovation's consequences. An organization's structure, which gives stability and continuity to the organization, often provides some powerful resistances to an innovation. Often, implementation of a new medium in an organization has been ignored or underemphasized, leading to problems in getting the innovation adopted and used.

There can be considerable flexibility in implementing an innovation. Formative evaluation helps fit the innovation into the organizational context in which it will be used. This can include the process of "re-invention," where new uses are discovered for an already-existing technology (Rice and Rogers, 1980). Exactly how to modify an innovation to fit it best into the existing organization and its perceived problems is a matter for which formative evaluation can be ideally suited. New media such as electronic messaging systems, computer bulletin boards, and videotext systems usually encounter severe problems at the implementation stage. Many of these problems could be avoided, or at least minimized, if formative evaluation had been used when planning the implementation process.

What is formative evaluation? What is the conceptual and philosophical basis of formative evaluation? How is it done? Why hasn't formative evaluation been used more often when implementing a new medium? This chapter seeks to answer these questions.

Characteristics of Formative Evaluation

BACKGROUND

One reason for some of the current misconceptions about formative evaluation, and for its lack of widespread use, is the recency of its origins. Formative evaluation, as a concept, has not been around long. Nevertheless, a major trend toward such evaluation has occurred. Why this movement toward evaluation in recent years?

The term *formative evaluation* was coined only in 1967, although such research by different names has been going on for a long time (Cambre, 1981). The event that gave formative evaluation its big push was the beginning of the popular children's television program "Sesame Street" in 1967–68. This program was expensive, had impact, and was wide-reaching (about 40 percent of all U.S. children aged two to five watch "Sesame Street" every day). One reason for its effectiveness was traced to the unique way in which it was produced: A joint team of television producers and formative evaluators at the Children's Television Workshop in New York worked together to make each program segment. For example, once a three-minute segment of a future "Sesame Street" program was initially produced, it would be shown to small test audiences of children to measure their degree of attention, how much they learned from it, and so on. Then the team of producers/evaluators would return to the television studio to redo the program segment. Sometimes, a three-minute segment might be redone, evaluated again, redone again, and so on through numerous cycles of production and evaluation. Considerable expense in time and money was obviously required by this process. But as a result, "Sesame Street" was dynamite with the targeted audience of U.S. children—and children abroad, when "Sesame Street" was broadcast in Spanish, German, Arabic, and other languages (with proper adaptation to these other cultures).

EVALUATION AS A RESEARCH FOCUS

Most textbooks about communication research, or about journalism, broadcasting, and film, do not mention formative evaluation. Therefore, it is not surprising that very little formative evaluation is conducted in the area of communication. Formative evaluation may be especially lacking in the case of the new media, where it might be particularly useful.

Most communication messages are not subjected to formative evaluation as a means of improving their effectiveness. On the rare occasions when a communication message or product has been pretested, the results of such formative evaluation are often ignored, if not strongly resisted, by message/product producers, who may regard such evaluation as interfering with their artistic and creative license and, worse, as threatening. Formative evaluation cannot only improve the effectiveness of messages, it can also be used to design and improve entire communication systems, although this application of formative evaluation seldom has been made.

Evaluation studies, which use scientific research methods, are one type of research carried out to measure the outcomes of activities or systems under operating conditions; they also provide a scientific basis for the decisions made by the individuals responsible for the effectiveness of the activities or systems. The distinctive aspect of evaluation is the purpose for which it is done—that is, evaluation research is conducted to determine the effects of plans, existing or potential activities, and systems on their direct participants. When we produce a message, we should always keep our audience in mind and be as specific as possible. We know of one author who pinned photographs of four individuals above his writing desk. They represented, to him, the audience for his book. Not just college sophomores, but particular sophomores in that author's course.

Use of formative evaluation is another way to be specific about one's audience. If the writer had pretested his manuscript with twenty or thirty sophomores, the feedback would have been much more reliable and empirical than it would be just thinking about one particular student as part of the intended audience. *Pretesting* is a type of formative evaluation that is designed to try out a communication message/system on its intended audience to refine its effectiveness prior to its widespread implementation. It is one type of formative evaluation that allows a message-maker to learn about an audience.

Formative evaluation is less concerned with the generalizability of the results than is other evaluative research. Of course, formative evaluators want to have some basis for generalizing their results to an intended audience, but they are usually willing to sacrifice some of the precision of generalizing from a sample to a population in exchange for other desired ends, like gaining an in-depth understanding of why a communication message or product is not effective with a small sample of receivers. Also, time is usually limited in a formative evaluation study.

The generalizability (from a sample to a population) of pretest results, and the precision of measurement, are usually not the main considerations in formative evaluation. Often, the formative evaluator is more concerned with gaining insight into how the message or product or system will affect an intended audience. Nothing should interfere with this desire to understand an audience's reactions to the message or product or system.

Formative as Against Summative Evaluation

We have already introduced the main distinction between formative and summative evaluation. In a major respect, this distinction depends on when the research is undertaken relative to the product or technology development. *Formative evaluation* is conducted while an activity, process, or system is ongoing in order to improve its effectiveness (Rogers, 1979). It is conducted "in-process," while the activity or system is still in some stage of design or development, so that the activity or system can be revised as a result of the corrective feedback. In contrast, *summative evaluation* is a type of research that is conducted to reach a decision about the effectiveness of an activity, process, or system after it has been developed and introduced. Such evaluation determines whether a fully developed message, product, or program has met its objectives. So summative evaluation is a means of looking backward to reach a judgment, but one that may affect the future, of course, if the message, process, or system is to be repeated.

The "early-warning" nature of formative evaluation, because of its timeliness, is a basic reason why it can be so valuable. Debugging of a new communication medium is very expensive and frustrating once a large, complex, and costly system is installed and once organizational procedures are established. At that point, an evaluation is too late.

The formative evaluator must be sure that the in-process feedback is provided when it is needed.

For summative research, the evaluator wishes to be as careful as possible in determining the truth-claims that are offered about the overall effects of a communication technology. The evaluator also usually has the luxury of a longer time period before his or her results are needed by decision makers. Summative evaluation can more closely parallel other types of research in the scientific rigor of its methods and thus in the accuracy of its results. In comparison, formative evaluations often must use smaller and/or nonrandom samples, less-structured measures, and less-sophisticated data-analysis.

This greater haste and lesser rigor of formative evaluation leads some communication scholars to falsely downgrade formative evaluation as "just like other research, but sloppy." We disagree. The objective of formative evaluation is different from other types of communication research; thus it cannot be fairly judged by those other standards, which were established for other purposes. Not only is formative evaluation often perceived as a less prestigious type of research than is summative evaluation (because the methods of investigation for formative evaluation are less "hard"), but both types of evaluation are perceived as less prestigious than is nonevaluation research. "Evaluators are looked down on as the drones of the research fraternity, technicians drudging away on dull issues and compromising their integrity out in the corrupt world" (Weiss, 1972, p. 9). On the other hand, Robert LaRose (1980) makes a strong case for the importance of formative research for mass communication research and theory, a point we return to later in this chapter.

PRACTICAL BENEFITS

The literature of formative evaluation contains many examples of the practical value of conducting early formative evaluation in a media project. Following are some examples:

- "Sesame Street"'s formative research showed early on that some of the attention-getting techniques of television commercial production (e.g., repetition, quick editing cuts, high interest figures) could be transferred into the production of educational television materials (Palmer, 1974).
- In the Children's Television Workshop series "3-2-1 Contact,"

Mielke and Chen (1983) showed that children were attracted to the realistic and often serious format of scientific investigation, a key premise for eventual production of that science series.

- "Carrascolendas," a bilingual television series for children of preschool through third grade, was originally developed for language drills. However, after formative evaluation showed the delight with which Mexican-American children reacted to television images of bilingual Spanish- and English-speaking children, the series was expanded to include self-concept and social objectives (Williams, LaRose & Frost, 1982).

- In a study of children's attitudes toward personal computers (models circa 1978) after a first day of Saturday computer camp, the researchers (Williams, Coulombe & Lievrouw, 1983) noted that several of the perceptions held by children about small computers were distinctively different from their adult teachers, and that there were gender differences in confidence about working with computers. For example, the children were not impressed with the small size or low costs of the machines as they had no point of reference to experience with other machines. Also, they took computers more for granted than the instruction anticipated (after all, computers had been in existence all the children's lives!). These differences were then the basis for an early revision of the camp curriculum.

Most of the above benefits would not have been realized if the research had not been undertaken early in the developmental process and if there were not clear lines of communication to the production or project developers. This point illustrates the practicalities of formative research projects where the researcher may move early and quickly to gain preliminary, yet practical, results. Certainly, there is some sacrifice of precision and thoroughness in such studies, but the practical benefits are important. Flay and Cook (1981) weigh the decisions of early "one-shot" formative evaluations as against longer term, "more careful path" studies in the use of mass media in health communication campaigns.

USES WITH NEW MEDIA

Formative evaluation seems especially relevant to the following applications involving new media: (1) the adoption of a new communication technology, (2) the types of communication behaviors people engage in with that technology, and (3) newly developed content or program materials for the systems. Most of the existing literature on formative evaluation fits within the third category, as do, for example, the studies of educational television development mentioned above and the use of videodisc with cancer patients (Van Tassel, 1987; also Chapter 11). However, we should expect to see increasing numbers of studies in the first two categories. Those in the first category would be extensions of diffusion or implementation studies where the adoption of an innovation paradigm (Rogers, 1983) is extended to include a new communication technology. Those in the second category are reflected in studies such as Steinfield's (1986) study of the use of electronic mail systems, although it was not expressly for formative evaluation purposes.

Steps in Formative Evaluation

1. DEFINE OBJECTIVES

Most formative research projects begin with definitions of intended behaviors or outcomes of what is to be evaluated. This procedure is largely a carryover from the concern with instructional objectives in educational research. In most of the large educational television projects mentioned in this chapter, the educational planners had developed a set of defined outcomes such that if the media materials were effective, these outcomes would be measurable in the students undertaking the course or program.

For example, in the "Freestyle" television project (Williams, LaRose & Frost, 1981), the overall goal was to lessen the biases of sex-role stereotypes when nine- to twelve-year-old students discussed adult occupations. Accordingly, an important instructional objective was that students understood the concept of sex-role stereotypes. In the early development of the series, long before any scenes were written or taped, there were detailed discussions of how this objective could be defined and later achieved with television material. One approach was to identify those occupations where students were likely to feel that only men or women would want to work in them (i.e., the stereotypes)—for example, women as nurses, men as truck drivers. Early ("baseline") research with children from the desired age group was conducted to see which occupations they tended to sex-role stereotype. Loosening these stereotypes then became an objective equally interpretable to the educational planners, the production team, and the formative researchers. Practically speaking, the television program would be successful if children ceased to assert that certain of the occupations were male or female "only." A few short scenes were written and produced that poked fun at stereotyping of these occupations, and then clips were shown in classrooms where children saw the materials and then discussed stereotypes. Although it was clear such video clips could be used to loosen sex-role stereotypes, after seeing four or five clips in sequence, the young students began to take the materials less seriously, thus destroying their effectiveness. This information was invaluable to the educational planner and producers who then modified their strategies for intervention.

A current project of one of the present authors (Williams, in progress) is intended to create a computer laboratory environment for university students where they can easily enter essays or papers they are writing, and then gain editorial feedback from the system (AT&T's Writers' Workbench—Collegiate Edition). A critical consideration is that students with no prior computer knowledge be able to sit at a computer terminal and easily operate the system. This objective lent itself to formative-type research beginning with small groups of students who were invited to try out the computer system. The questions or problems they raised were recorded, as were data from a post-use questionnaire. At several stages, the terminal screen presentation was altered to avoid noted problems, and a brief written handout was developed to answer the most often asked questions. Eventually, through this formation evaluation process, it was possible to achieve the objective of a nearly trouble-free self-introduction to the system.

Again, well-defined objectives are especially important as they are often the critical meeting-ground for the project planners, creative or design team, and the evaluators.

2. SELECT THE SCOPE OF THE RESEARCH

As mentioned in the introduction to this chapter, the scope of formative research may vary from small, informal studies to a large-scale program of schedule evaluations, as in television pilot programs.

In both the "Carrascolendas" and "Freestyle" projects, the chief formative researcher (Williams) had three responsibilities. One was to provide baseline data about the designated student population. For example, as described above, what sex role stereotypes did the boys hold toward certain occupations? This involved not only replicating portions of earlier studies but designing studies relative to the objectives of the television series. Baseline data would then be a starting point for studying behavior change. A second responsibility was to respond to requests for small, *ad hoc* studies, some with an overnight turnaround time. For example, video clips of two actors trying out for a single part might be tested on a small group of children. A tape recording of a song composed for a program might be tested for its appeal and comprehension. Or a storyboard of a proposed scene might be shown to teachers for their comments. Beyond these studies was a third responsibility of carrying out a formal plan for evaluation of pilot programs. These had a larger time frame, perhaps of a month or so, where programs would be taken into the field and evaluated as prototypes for the series.

The new media often present special challenges, as illustrated in the videodisc project for counseling cancer patients' relatives and friends (Van Tassel, 1987). The sample size in a formative evaluation study is often smaller than in other types of research. Van Tassel pretested her interactive videodisc program for hair loss due to radiation treatment of cancer with only a handful of respondents because each pretest required several hours.

Because of the interactive nature of the videodisc technology, each respondent could follow any one of a thousand idiosyncratic paths through the videodisc program (which is like a multitude of videotape segments, each dealing with a particular aspect of hair loss due to cancer). The investigator wanted to know how understandable each of the segments was to the intended users, and how understandable any particular sequence of such segments might be. Thus, instead of formatively evaluating a single message (like a poster or a news article), Van Tassel was evaluating a wide variety of combinations of possible messages.

One can easily appreciate just how much more complicated formative evaluation becomes when the medium being evaluated is highly interactive.

3. SELECT DATA-GATHERING METHOD

Although formative evaluation is one type of research, evaluation methods are not necessarily identical to traditional research methods.

The reason for this difference lies in the purpose of research and of evaluation. The objective of research is to provide new knowledge that is universally valid. In contrast, evaluation is usually conducted to provide a basis for decisions about the effectiveness of activities or systems. This latter objective means that speed is often an important consideration in formative studies—for example, data need to be gathered and analyzed rapidly. Otherwise, there is no time to use the results as a basis for planning the next step of a project.

Formative data-gathering methods include:

1. Observation
2. Group interviews
3. Individual questionnaires and personal interviews
4. Recall tests
5. Rankings
6. Pretesting
7. Physiological responses

We often mix data-gathering methods, to use back-up tests or questionnaires with individual or panel interviews. A multimeasurement approach is almost always more accurate, insightful, and comprehensive than any single technique, so many formative evaluation researchers follow a triangulation strategy (Chapter 3). The formative evaluation conducted for the children's science show "3-2-1 Contact" was perhaps the most comprehensive of triangulation researches, as Mielke and Chen (1983) used nearly twenty different pretesting approaches as a formal part of their design. The earlier mentioned "Freestyle" project provides an excellent example of the value of multiple measures or observations. Although young boys would unequivocally declare on formal questionnaires that certain occupations were "not for women," they appeared far less rigid in their stereotypes in follow-up focus group discussions. For example, when asked why women would not be truck drivers, a typical response was that trucks were too difficult to load or steer. When it was pointed out that most trucks have power steering or many do not require the drivers to load them (e.g., a gasoline truck), boys would often reply that in those cases there probably would be no problem for women drivers.

A similar experience is often encountered when people are introduced to computers or some other new communication technology. They may declare their noninterest in, or even fear of, the technology. Yet in an informal discussion, one may find that it is fear of

personal embarrassment, change of status in an organization, or
change in daily work routines that worries them most. Accordingly,
formative research on technology adoption often suggests that training or orientation concentrate as much on defusing these attitudes as
upon how to operate the technology.

4. ANALYZE RESULTS AND PROVIDE FEEDBACK

Well-executed traditional methods of data-analysis and reporting—
with due concern for validity and reliability—are as important in
formative studies as they are in any other. However, the need for
speed as well as the challenge of communicating results to individuals
who are not research specialists often prompt innovations in analyzing
and presenting the results of formative research. We present several
examples here.

One advantage of studying new communication technology is that
the systems themselves often provide a basis for data-gathering
(Chapter 6) and easy display of results. For example, in the study of
the computer-based writing laboratory, a small program was
eventually entered where, after students had used the system for a
full session, they were branched to a brief computerized questionnaire. In this respect the system now maintains an ongoing formative
evaluation component that can be readily consulted by the laboratory
administrators.

Media production projects are especially challenging because it is
important to cast results into a format the creative team can interpret.
Tables of numbers or complex graphs may go unheeded by all except
the research-oriented personnel on a project. Some of the major
educational media projects have developed innovations for meeting
this challenge. For example, in the "Freestyle" project, major segments from pilot films were evaluated by groups of about a hundred
children in auditoriums equipped with audience response meters. In
one mode, these meters could be operated like a continuous dial with
the two extreme positions defined to the audience as indicating extreme like versus dislike of the materials that they were viewing.
Prior to viewing the pilot films, the members of the audience were
given training and warm-up materials to help them become ac-
customed to the hand-held meters. This also made it possible to
validate their use of the system by seeing if their responses reflected
the showing of boring or high-interest warm-up materials.

Results of the metered evaluations could be interpreted in a variety of ways, some of which were immediately available to the creative team. For example:

- A computer display of the results could be viewed in "real-time" as the student-audience made their evaluations.
- A video recording of the computer display could be viewed at a later time and synchronized with the tape of the pilot programs.
- Digital results of the evaluations could be averaged and entered as marginal notes on the program scripts.

Many of the above alternatives, and others, could be easily improved given the ease by which computer graphics can now be generated. However, an even simpler procedure, one without the audience meters, proved useful in the "Freestyle" project. This method was to videotape audience responses to the program, and then to edit this image into a small quarter-frame in synchronization with the original program. This was popular with the creative staff, as were videotapes (rather than written notes) of focus-group discussions.

Which of the above approaches is preferred? Probably a *combination* is the best answer, especially where different response measures or records provide a triangulation of results.

Formative Evaluation as Mass Communications Research

Despite the value of formative evaluation as a type of communication research, there is an attitude that it may be so practically oriented as not to merit serious attention as a contribution to theory or a type of research important in an advanced student's graduate training. Robert LaRose (1980), himself an experienced formative researcher, summarizes an excellent case for the importance of formative research to mass communication theory. Although this narrows the topic to media content studies, his position is an interesting conclusion for this chapter, for there can be more to formative methods than designing products or encouraging adoption.

For one, LaRose argued that the consideration of formative studies when applied to the mass media suggests a theoretical position that the mass media can, indeed, have discernible, specific effects. This is counter to the "weak effects" theoretical position advanced, for example, by Klapper (1960), wherein the effects of mass media are seen as more indirect than direct, as in the two-step flow theory or in the agenda-setting process. Formative studies that have shown media producers, strategies for increasing specific effects can lend theoretical insight into the characteristics of such media—as, for example, developed over the years for "Sesame Street." LaRose argued that the reason so many mass media may have limited effects is that their messages are poorly designed, a point made earlier by Fishbein and Ajzen (1975) when they outlined their model of how social expectancies as related to media messages may have persuasive power. LaRose proposed that formative researchers can benefit by more attention to theoretical models in mass communication and persuasion research.

An important concluding point to this chapter, therefore, is that formative evaluation should not be relegated only to the category of a *practical* tool kit in message development studies. On the contrary, formative evaluation should be among the strategies for contributing to theory, not only to mass media theory but to the adoption and effects of new communication media.

Summary

Formative evaluation is used mainly as a developmental form of research where feedback is given to the media or technology developers. It has been most often used in education and frequently in large educational television projects—for example, "Sesame Street." This type of evaluation may range from informal *ad hoc* studies to a more formal plan to conduct developmental evaluations throughout a project.

Formative evaluation is often distinguished from summative evaluation, or the study of a technology or media product once it is completed and in the field.

Many practical benefits can be gained from formative evaluation, including making editorial or production adjustments in media products or studying the implementation process for new communication technologies. An example of a new media application described in this chapter involved the use of a videodisc program for counseling cancer patients and their relatives and friends.

Steps in formative evaluation include: (1) define objectives, (2) select the scope of the research, (3) select the data-gathering method, and (4) analyze results and provide feedback.

Finally, an argument was made for the importance of formative evaluation as a method of mass communication research.

CHAPTER 9

Evaluating Costs and Benefits

Return on Investment

All new media involve financial investments for implementation, and sooner or later questions arise about the return on that investment. In other words, what are the benefits gained relative to the costs invested? This question may be raised for a single implementation, such as equipping an office with an upgraded word-processing system. One might ask about a larger implementation, like the installation of computers to assist in the teaching of reading throughout a school district. Or a still larger implementation might be the investment in a cellular radio system for a metropolitan area.

One of the fundamental premises regarding investment in communication media systems is that while the costs of labor and materials have consistently risen over the last several decades, the costs of technology have decreased. Figure 9–1 illustrates this trend. The objective in many applications of communication media investment is to make a "cost trade-off" from the more to the less expensive alternative on these curves.

In this chapter, we examine the general methods for cost-benefit analyses. A more detailed analysis of such methods for the evaluation of information systems is provided by Sassone (1988). These methods are especially valuable in an era when it is frequently asked whether the expected benefits of new technologies are worth the added investment. Calculating a ratio of costs to likely returns provides a basis for comparing the gains (or losses) from a technology investment relative to existing practices, or for comparing different investment alter-

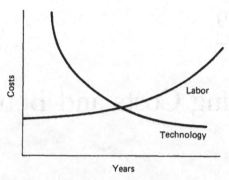

Figure 9–1. Generalized Illustration of Labor vs. Technology Cost Tradeoffs

natives. These methods are valuable not only for formal research but as a management tool.

After discussing some of the bases for cost-benefits analysis, we examine three examples that also illustrate different levels of application. These include a library cataloging system, use of educational television in a Third World country, and the predicted benefits of telecommuncations investments in an African nation.

Methods for Costs Analyses

TYPES OF ANALYSES

Analyzing costs relative to effects typically takes one of four forms. The following definitions reflect most of the usual usage of cost analysis terminology as well as the definitions proposed by Levin (1983) on the topic. Still, however, one will frequently see the labels used interchangeably. The two best-known analyses are:

> *Cost-benefits:* A ratio of the monetary value of an investment divided by the monetary value of expected benefits.
> *Cost-effectiveness:* The monetary cost of an investment relative to the measure of a nonmonetary outcome.

Added to the above are analyses reflecting more generally on the desirability of an investment or whether it is feasible at all. These include:

> *Cost utility:* The monetary amount of investment relative to some qualitative condition that is a valued outcome.

Cost feasibility: The evaluation of costs to determine if the invest-ments are within the means of the individual organization.

Most cost analyses are interpreted in a relative sense—that is, the comparison of one alternative with another. Although a knowledge of some type of cost benefits ratio is itself significant, its use as a decision criterion typically involves examining differences between or among different ratios. But relative to what? This is the key question in most of these types of analyses, meaning that we do not just calculate costs relative to benefits for a single investment but compare it to some alternative investment. For example, in investing in a new telephone system for an office, one might compare the known monthly cost per call of the existing phone system relative to the estimated monthly cost of the new one. The key question is whether the cost-benefit ratio improves. In terms of cost feasibility, certain alternatives may be possible to consider while others are beyond the budget of the organization.

APPLICATIONS TO NEW MEDIA

As useful as cost studies might seem, there are few examples in the literature for new media technologies. There are studies where cost is considered, but a formal cost effectiveness evaluation is seldom seen. One reason for the lack of literature on this topic is that although costs are usually deemed important in studies of communication media, most evaluation studies have looked more into effects on performance than into studying performance relative to cost. For example, the implementation of word processing in an office may be studied in terms of changes in secretarial output, attitudes, or benefits to the organization, but a detailed assessment relative to cost, particularly cost-investment alternatives, is seldom found (Johnson & Rice, 1987).

Another consideration is that when one attempts to isolate the specific benefits or payoff of a new media investment, the analysis becomes more detailed than a cost-benefits perspective. This is the consideration of productivity, the subject of Chapter 10.

Example: Assessing Educational Television

In the 1960s, when one author (Williams) was conducting research for the U.S. Office of Economic Opportunity, the prospects for using television as a powerful new educational tool seemed remarkably bright. "Sesame Street" was soon to enjoy a national, then international, success. Memos were circulated among policymakers extolling the possibilities of bringing the best of teachers and curriculum to children at the cost of only pennies per child. Research consistently showed that televised lessons could result in learning gains almost always equal to, or even exceeding, "live" classes. These qualities made television a promising alternative for producing and rapidly disseminating instructional materials in Third World countries. Yet as the years passed, the prospects of educational television grew dim. It just simply did not live up to its many promises. Production costs of high-quality educational television were substantial, often more than school systems, including those in Third World countries, could afford. Most instruction, for children at least, required a "live" teacher and classroom environment to be effective as an overall educational system. Television alone was not enough. For a comprehensive educational curriculum, television was better seen as a complement to classroom instruction, a technique to make teachers more effective.

Most early studies of educational television did not take the costs of associated classrooms and local teachers into account. They compared the benefits of instruction (e.g., gains in test scores) while not fully examining the costs of the television alternative. As it turned out, television was eventually recognized as a costly instructional alternative, at least relative to what could be achieved by making similar, lower level investments in upgrading teachers and curricula without the television component. Popular literature accused teachers of being resistant, or television producers of being uncreative. But a powerful reason, as illustrated in a study to be described next, was that when costs were balanced against benefits, and comparisons were made among educational alternatives, a more precise evaluation of television media investments raised questions of their worth. The idea of comparison among alternatives is a key point in the evaluation of cost-benefits.

For years, economist and educational researcher Martin Carnoy (1975) had been very concerned that investments in educational television for Third World countries had been too highly touted and too little evaluated. His study of educational television in El Salvador illustrates the "relative-to-what" issues in cost studies of the new media.

Ideally, educational television should be an efficient means for rapidly disseminating the best of educational content and teaching strategies to a large population. But on closer inspection, important issues must be considered. For example, there are the high costs of educational equipment and curriculum development for educational television and the skilled staff that is required. Both funding and expertise are scarce resources in Third World countries. Professor Carnoy was concerned that the costs of educational television were not being closely enough examined, especially as compared to instructional alternatives.

Carnoy analyzed data on the implementation of educational television systems and on comparative investments in curriculum development and improved teacher training. At the time of his research in the early 1970s, little evaluation had been conducted on the costs of educational television relative to the presumed benefits. Most research just measured television's effects on learning gains based on standardized tests, then compared these to test scores for traditional classes in the same subjects where no new media were used.

Carnoy analyzed cost data for three methods of instruction in mathematics, science, and social science. The methods were:

1. Traditional classroom
2. Revised curriculum, improved teacher training
3. Revised curriculum, improved teacher training plus use of televised lessons

If Carnoy's study had been conducted as in most past research, the results of the televised instruction would have been compared only to traditional classrooms. There would be ambiguity about whether test score differences were due to the television treatment or to the revised curriculum and teacher training. To improve the research design of the El Salvador study, special control groups were formed with all the characteristics of the television classes, except that television was not used. Benefits were measured by scores on standardized tests in the three subject-matter areas.

Table 9–1 summarizes results of the study conducted during 1968–72 in El Salvador. It compares gains in test scores for the three treatments. As can be seen in this table, both the television and the control classes had substantial gains over traditional teaching methods for mathematics and social studies. The gains of the television classes exceeded those of the control group except in science, where the control group exceeded the educational television classes.

Was the investment in educational television the best alternative? Not really. On closer inspection, we should question whether the added expense of television was worth the investment. Accordingly,

Table 9–1. Results of an Experiment on Educational Television in El Salvador Elementary Schools

Subject	Gain in Test Scores (Feb.–Oct.)	Gain in Test Scores Over Traditional Teaching
Mathematics:		
1. For traditional classes	1.95	. . .
2. For experiment ETV classes	5.70	3.7
3. For experiment control group (reform but no ETV)	5.20	3.2
Science:		
1. For traditional classes	1.34	. . .
2. For experiment ETV classes	4.20	2.9
3. For experiment control group (reform but no ETV)	5.10	3.8
Social studies:		
1. For traditional classes	2.61	. . .
2. For experiment ETV classes	6.40	3.8
3. For experiment control group (reform but no ETV)	3.10	1.5

SOURCE: Carnoy (1975, p. 237); used by permission of the publisher.

it is useful to compare the test score results in a cost-benefits paradigm as shown in Table 9–2. Here the average cost per student in the educational television classes was $22—$6 more than in the control reform classes. In other words, the basic cost of the improved curriculum and training was $16, and the added cost of the television component was $6. Note that when costs are considered, the control version of the instruction is more cost-beneficial than the educational television version for mathematics or science. For social studies, the benefits still favor the educational television system.

Table 9–2. Cost-Effectiveness Ratios for Educational Television and for Reform-Only in El Salvador

Subject	Educational TV	Reform Only
Mathematics	3.7/$22 = 0.17	3.2/$16 = 0.20
Science	2.9/$22 = 0.13	3.8/$16 = 0.24
Social studies	3.8/$22 = 0.17	1.5/$16 = 0.10

SOURCE: Carnoy (1975, p. 238); used by permission of the publisher.

Carnoy used these results and those from similar analyses in other Third World countries to question whether the added expense of educational television was a worthwhile investment. Frequently, curriculum revision and teacher training involving educational television projects was itself enough of a boost to instructional gains that the added cost of the television component was not justified. Carnoy recognized that television could improve instruction on a much broader scale than curriculum reform alone. On the other hand, training teachers was itself a better long-range investment than was television equipment.

Carnoy's analysis not only lent insights from a cost-benefits evaluation of educational television, but it was a basis for setting more detailed standards for new educational media projects. If evaluated in cost-benefits terms, the results of an investment in educational television can be determined more precisely than if only learning gains are examined. This general lesson from the El Salvador project carries over to investment decisions in new communication media in almost any application where gains can be compared relative to costs.

Example: Assessing a Computerized Card Cataloging System

As you may have already experienced from using on-line card catalogs, libraries are a major adopter of communication technologies. The investments are also found behind the scenes in the form of computer-assisted cataloging systems. When a book enters a library's collection, it must be "cataloged"—that is, assigned its Library of Congress number and entered into the library's records in author, title, and subject files. This is a type of operation that lends itself well to computer assistance. Presumably, there would be cost advantages if the labor-intensive aspects of this operation were computerized.

An analysis of a computer-assisted "on-line shared cataloging system" conducted by Morita and Gapen (1977) at Ohio State University illustrates the application of cost-benefits calculations to this type of technological implementation. Although the details of the study are more than we need to go into here, various features of the on-line system were implemented from 1970 to 1975, the period of their study. Several important considerations were acknowledged in their research. For one, it was not possible to make a straightforward comparison between manual and on-line cataloging because components of the system, as with many different types of communication technologies, were phased in over a period of time. Further, development of the system required certain changes in library organization and procedures that were bound to influence results. Finally, so that cost figures could be realistically compared, it was necessary to adjust all data to reflect the annual inflation rate (based on the Consumer Price Index). Table 9–3 shows a sample of the type of results obtained in the study, the basic unit costs (total titles/total costs) of cataloging titles for five time-period (six months except for 1975, which was three) samples within the five years. The implementation was begun in late 1970.

The sample of results shown in Table 9–3 suggest a generalization that was found throughout the study: There is an initial higher cost of media implementation that must be accommodated before realizing the eventual benefits. Presumably, this initial cost results from the organization's adjustment to the new system, learning to take advantage of its benefits. It is also possible to use these figures to project costs into later years, or to set standards of performance.

Example: Assessing Expanded Telecommunications

There are also larger scale applications of cost-benefits analyses than described in the preceding sections. For example, one might wish to calculate the benefits of computerization of an entire industry or the return on investment generated by a new telecommunications network for an entire country. Because of their magnitude, these larger scale analyses lose precision. However, they are valuable in an era where many experts hold that communication media investment may offer the "competitive edge" of one business over another or even the development of one region of the country over another. The

Table 9–3. Sample of Costs Data Taken from Study of On-line Library Cataloging System

Year	Total Titles	Basic Unit Costs
1970	15,722	$8.30
1972	12,802	10.00
1973	12,600	7.51
1974	12,156	8.59
1975	5,609	7.90

SOURCE: Morita and Gapen (1977, p. 291).

present example of a large-scale analysis comes from a paper by Charles Jonscher (1985) originally presented at a National Science Foundation workshop on the relationship between telecommunications and national development. It also illustrates how cost-benefits analyses can be used for forecasting return on investment.

The objective in this research was to estimate cost-benefits of proposed telecommunications investments in Kenya, mainly in the Nairobi area. The rationale was that telecommunications benefits should be evaluated at a level beyond the services themselves—that is, telecommunications investment should be thought of as improving other businesses, and that should be the basis of the benefits calculation. A first focus, therefore, in the research was to identify specific categories of telecommunications benefits that could then be examined across various businesses. These included (Jonscher, 1985, pp. 23–24):

- *Business expansion:* By restricting a firm's access to customers, suppliers, or other producers, lack of effective telephone service may constrain the growth of that firm's business. Since most industrial operations experience economies of scale in production, expansion of output results in lower unit costs and greater efficiency.
- *Managerial time:* Enhanced and expanded telecommunications services can improve managerial efficiency and result in a need for fewer manager hours per unit of output.
- *Labor time:* There are many instances in which extra labor is employed to substitute for effective communication facilities. Personnel are employed as messengers, drivers, and sometimes guards, where security levels are low because of an inability to contact the police.
- *Inventory levels:* When production stops because of a machine breakdown, parts shortage, raw material deficiency, or for other reasons, communications problems are likely to add to the time elapsed before restart.
- *Vehicle fleet scheduling:* Management of vehicle movements is usually an information-intensive activity. Dispatching trucks, organizing their movement between geographically remote locations, and dealing with breakdowns all require extensive communication. Lack of access to telephone facilities leads to less efficient use of vehicles than could otherwise be achieved.

- *Purchasing decisions:* The process of buying supplies and raw materials at competitive prices requires access to much information. The advantage of the telephone in this context is that rapid transfer of price information is possible in a way no other medium can match.
- *Selling prices:* The reverse process, seeking out the highest possible selling prices, should be assessed in a similar way. The need to obtain the highest price proves to be particularly important in the export of agricultural products, where access to good price information is essential for the marketing of a perishable commodity subject to wide variations in supply.
- *Distribution costs:* There are many ways in which deficiencies in telecommunication services can increase overall costs. Some of these effects are accounted for under other headings discussed above. Others must be counted separately—for example, freight handling and transport contractors' charges, marketing costs, and the costs associated with running out of supplies at remote depots.

The foregoing types of benefits were analyzed in microeconomic case studies of nine major Kenyan businesses. Estimated values of the benefits were calculated as were the projected extra telecommunications costs to achieve those benefits. The results of these analyses are shown in Table 9–4.

The benefit ratios in this table are overly optimistic because they show a large return on investment. Part of the reason is that only telecommunications charges are entered into the costs side of the equation. Obviously, as more activities are generated because of increased telecommunications capabilities, other costs would have to be considered—for example, personnel. On the other hand, the cost-benefits paradigm is especially valuable as we ask harder questions about communication media investments. Too often it has been assumed that any new media investment will improve performance. Although that may often be the case, there is still the question of the degree to which the increased or new costs will be justified by the benefits (Chapter 10).

Somewhat similar studies are regularly conducted to calculate the return on investment as telephone or data networks are expanded. Observed usage of the network is recorded for different points in time and correlated with different characteristics of users and the circumstances of use. These data are then used to predict amounts of in-

Table 9–4. Cost-Benefits Estimates of Telecommunications
Improvements in Selected Kenyan Businesses

Nature of Business	Estimated Value of Benefits (Kenyan shillings × 1,000/yr.)	Telecommunications Charges	Benefits/Costs
Hotel chain	870	13.5	64.5
Newspaper	6036	31.1	194.3
Horticultural producer	27	2.5	10.7
Distributor	2380	17.0	139.9
Agricultural exporter	2628	31.5	83.5
Diversified manufacturer	11930	125.4	95.1
Freight transporter	5565	57.9	96.1
Travel agency	275	2.3	118.7
Food processing company	4418	14.8	299.3
Total or average	34128	296	115.3

SOURCE: C. Jonscher, "Assessing the Benefits of Telecommunications," *InterMedia*, vol. 13, no. 1, January 1985, p. 24; used by permission of the publisher.

creased revenues as a result of service increase on the expanded network. These increased revenues are then examined in a cost-benefits paradigm to forecast the likely return on investment or to compare different degrees or types of network expansion.

Major Steps in a Cost Analysis

1. DEFINE THE PROBLEM

A cost analysis should focus specifically on the problem under study, typically a research question or hypothesis. You do not necessarily start with something that is easy to measure. Most cost evaluations are based on comparisons; otherwise there is no relative basis for interpreting the research results. You must know that data needed for the analysis can be located or generated. There may be cases, especially in businesses, where management does not want to show communication media costs, especially if this information would be valuable to the competition. Some public organizations do not wish to publicize their expenditures for a new medium because they will risk being reported negatively if the desired benefits are not realized. In practical terms, costs data are sometimes hard to gather.

2. SELECT THE ANALYSIS METHOD

Although we have already described types of cost analyses, you might think of them in terms of the following examples:

- Can computer instruction labs be substituted for certain textbook costs? (cost feasibility)
- What are the priorities relative to costs for purchasing computer-assisted software for marketing, sales analysis, planning, accounting, and product design? (cost utility)
- Is videodisc a better investment for training new mechanics than videotape? (cost-effectiveness)
- Over a ten-year period, we hypothesize that there will be cost savings over traditional methods for an investment in an automated check-out counter for these ten retail stores. (cost-benefits)

Notice that most of the above problems reflect the "relative to what?" component. Although there may be cases where you mainly want to describe benefits or effectiveness, more often you will be making comparisons since a single cost analysis in isolation may leave little to interpret. So bear in mind that the *comparative* aspect of the focus of your study should be clear.

Much of what you may read about cost analyses was written to help practical decision makers. Remember that in the present approach we are mainly interested in research applications that describe, evaluate, or explain the cost consequences of new media or communication technologies.

3. GATHER DATA

Usually, the costs component offers the greatest challenge for quantification, especially the hidden costs. All costs necessary to create the service or product must be taken into account. It is as if all were being started from "scratch." Often, computer systems are purchased without the thought of software, maintenance, remodeling, furniture, consumable supplies, or personnel costs. Every possible detail of costs should be identified. If certain existing resources are being used (e.g., furniture), they must have some level of value that should be included in the analysis. It may even be important to calculate overhead costs of heating, lighting, and power. Investments in telecommunications often overlook tariff details.

Costs must be adjusted for a common time frame. If a new computer system is to be purchased, a common practice is to calculate a depreciation schedule (e.g., five years); this annual cost can then be further divided to fit the desired analysis. Space often presents a problem for cost analysis. The proportion or fraction of space often must be identified. The cost base of already-owned property can be estimated from the costs of a comparable rental. Or as with equipment, a life span of the building (e.g., fifty years) could be a basis for estimating an annual or monthly cost. Dollar values must also take into account different inflation rates over different periods, so that dollar values are comparable. Further, dollar values have an "opportunity cost"—that is, how much return will a given amount of funds generate over a given time period in *other* investments.

4. CONDUCT ANALYSIS AND DRAW CONCLUSIONS

The analyses and results may appear similar to those given earlier for the educational television study. Although cost analyses are often conducted for practical decision making, in more formal research projects the results should be mapped back onto the basic statement of the problem—that is, as a test of a hypothesis or answer to a research question or questions.

It may also be useful to consider uses of graphs or charts to communicate your conclusion. Further, in this era of easily used computer spreadsheets, you might include a series of "what if?" calculations showing how benefits may be affected as different cost components are varied.

Beyond Cost Analyses

Several times in this chapter we mentioned that cost figures could be used as a management tool. This is in an application usually called standards and variance of production. Suppose that, as the result of a costs study, you found that the average letter cost $1.92 a page to produce in a word-processing pool. In order to set costs standards, you might plot costs across time to see how samples would fluctuate about the mean. As illustrated in Figure 9–2, you could set $1.92 as a

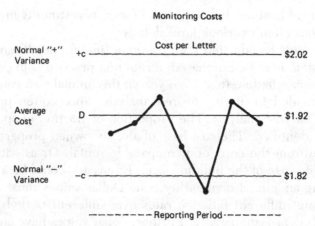

Figure 9–2. Hypothetical Example of Variances in Cost-Performance of a Word Processing System

production "standard" and plus or minus $0.10 as the normal fluctuation or "variance" you would expect. If values go outside this variance, especially above, you would take this as a sign that some trouble-shooting is needed.

For another managerial example, suppose that you upgraded your word-processing equipment in the hopes of cutting production costs. Unless you set new production standards, you might be caught in the old trap of "work expanding to fill the available time." Perhaps from the experience of others, you set a new production standard, then you could use cost studies and standards and variance analyses to evaluate your new investment. The important practical point is that improved cost performance may take more than just new media systems; it will take management to encourage the benefits. Of course, employee motivation and cooperation is critical for success. For example, the focus of the Johnson and Rice study (1987) was to identify those management implementation policies that led to innovative uses of word processing and enriched jobs, not just the use of the word processor to increase routine production.

Finally, before embarking on a cost analysis that takes one of the four forms defined in this chapter, consider whether the problem you are assessing goes beyond the basic measures of cost of production. If you are more concerned with the larger contribution of a media system to a business or organization, then alternative approaches such as productivity or value-added analyses may be of greater benefit. These are described in the following chapter.

Summary

Many media investments represent some type of cost trade-off among alternative investments, thus making cost-benefits analysis an increasingly important area of new media research. In many cases this trade-off substitutes technologies that have a downward cost trend with other machinery, labor, or both, which have an upward trend.

Methods for cost analyses include: cost-benefits, or the monetary ratio of investment and operation costs relative to value returned; cost effectiveness, or the ratio of costs to a measure of a nonmonetary return; cost utility, or the amount of investment relative to some qualitatively defined outcome; and cost feasibility, usually whether an organization can afford a given investment.

Several examples were given of cost analyses of new media or technologies, including educational television in El Salvador, the computerization of a card cataloging system for a library, and telecommunications investments in Kenyan businesses.

Major steps in a cost analysis include: (1) define the problem, (2) select the analysis method, (3) gather data, and (4) conduct the analysis and draw conclusions.

It was also noted that cost analyses many enter into larger scale evaluations of business or organizational effectiveness, including productivity, and value-added analyses, both discussed in Chapter 10.

Measuring Productivity

Going Beyond Costs and Benefits

Back in the 1960s, an IBM salesman worked hard to convince a Midwestern manufacturer of crop-drying equipment to computerize his accounting office. The sales representative argued beyond a doubt that accounting costs could be cut by 50 percent based on the amortization of a $50,000 computer investment over five years. The manufacturer, being a keen business executive, noted that even if this were true, it would have little effect on his overall business. Accounting only reflected about 2 percent of his costs of doing business. He later found that the same $50,000, when expended for a computer to aid in manufacturing control, decreased his manufacturing costs by about 10 percent. Since his manufacturing costs were nearly two thirds of the costs of running his business, the gain from this computer investment increased profits by several hundred thousand dollars. Moreover, these gains improved his competitive position in the crop-drying equipment market.

On a detailed level, we could calculate cost-benefits of either of the above alternative computer investments, yet of more importance is the relative effect of these investments on the overall business. We could, for example, enter these alternatives into an analysis of the overall costs of doing business relative to the revenues returned from product sales. Since the ratio of revenues to costs would be greater for the manufacturing investment than the accounting one, the former choice would be more "productive." And productivity ratios, like cost-benefit ratios, could be calculated if desired. Furthermore, we could calculate a ratio between the costs of using the computers in manufacturing and the revenues minus all other costs to gain an index of the contribution of the computer investment to running the business. This concept is known as "value added." Productivity and value-added analyses look more at a business as a whole and are thus valuable for seeing the larger scale contributions of communication media investments. As we later discuss, value-added analyses can be especially helpful when assessing the competitive position of a business relative to others.

In this chapter we examine these larger scale analyses, including their usefulness in studying media system investments as offering a competitive advantage—that is, as a strategic investment for the business or nonprofit organization. We add "organization" here, because productivity is certainly as important to nonprofit or social service organizations as it is to profit-making enterprises (Holzer & Halachmi, 1986).

Productivity as Efficiency Ratios

BASIC PRODUCTION RATIOS

The basic approach to measuring productivity is the ratio of output to input, or an efficiency formula:

$$\text{Efficiency} = \text{input/output}$$

This estimate of efficiency, like cost-benefits, is often thought of as a "factory analogy." For example, suppose that the current cost of maintaining a data clerk and equipment for entering transactions were $100 per day and the number of transactions were 1,000; the cost is thus 10 cents per transaction. If, without adding any costs, the output were increased to 1,200 transactions per day, the cost per transaction would be reduced to 8.3 cents, or a 17 percent increase in efficiency. These types of productivity gains from new communication systems are at the "unit-processing" level of analysis, as in the number of keystrokes per hour, letters written per day, phone calls switched per hour, or computing in terms of "instructions per second."

One common but generally narrow dimension of the value of new communication systems may sometimes be estimated in this simple formula. Suppose you needed a $5,000 computer (including maintenance and interest costs) to gain the extra 200 transactions per day. If you annualized the cost of the computer on a five-year depreciation schedule for 250 workdays per year, you add $4 per day to your costs. But costs per transaction would be 8.7 cents, still an advantage over the former rate of 10 cents per transaction. Note that we included interest costs in the simplified $5,000 figure. It is important to bear in mind that the cost of money—its "opportunity cost"—is always an important factor in these types of calculations. There are also considerations in terms of current tax laws, including depreciation schedules, which have changed in recent years. These latter factors, all of which affect costs, may make the difference between a favorable and unfavorable investment in business equipment or systems.

However, these efficiency calculations have several shortcomings when one examines investments in communication media relative to the overall business or enterprise. For one, although the simple counting of units of output for a work-station may be an index of productivity, its value to the business may be unknown. Let us take a negative example: Suppose the business seldom needed to process over 1,000 transactions per day. The added cost of the computer would boost the existing cost per transaction from 10 cents to 10.4 cents if only 1,000 transactions were done per day. This would represent lost money due to the unused capacity of the computer (a common occurrence). Also, the employee who might otherwise be taking a full workday for 1,200 units is likely finishing earlier with only 1,000 to do (unless they let the work expand to fill the available time, another common occurrence). So unless that employee's extra time is spent on some other productive activity for the business, there is a loss there too.

The point here is more obvious than it might seem in a simple productivity analysis. For expanded capacity to offer a return on investment to a business, (1) the market must be able to return revenues for the extra products or services, (2) the unused (displaced) capacity of workers or equipment must be employed productively on some other task in the organization, or (3) both.

It may be more important to know the value that a new communication system adds to a business, not just the increase in output units. For example, the increase to 1,200 transactions per day might allow a business to collect its receivables (money due) 10 percent faster than before. This change might be gauged in thousands of dollars in cash flow or a reduction in overhead of the costs of borrowing money. The ratio of change in either impact variable might be a high percentage of efficiency gain as compared with cost-savings on the transaction process alone.

Another problem with the simple efficiency formula is that as one moves away from clerical to managerial levels of an organization, the output side of the equation may not be so easily quantified. Suppose, for example, that an executive makes better decisions because of a computerized decision-support system. How will that improvement be quantified? Just the number or speed of decisions may be misleading because an executive might be involved in eight minor poor decisions and one major critical one. One must identify as carefully as possible where the value is added by the new communication technology and attempt to capture that value on the output side of the equation. Many times this is nearly impossible or misleading in a simple efficiency formula.

RATIOS OF REVENUES RELATIVE TO PERSONNEL OR TECHNOLOGY

Perhaps you have read where two companies are compared on the basis of a ratio of revenues relative to employees. A company with 25,000 employees generating $500 million annually in gross revenues has a revenue ratio of $20,000 per employee. If all other factors are equal, this company is more efficient than a company generating only $15,000 per employee. You often see such figures in descriptions of U.S. agriculture, which is highly mechanized. An American farm worker may produce ten to fifty times more wheat than a counterpart in a less-developed country.

The same reasoning is a key issue concerning investment in new communication media. For example, does the contribution of computer expenses sufficiently increase employee productivity to not only cover the computer costs but also to boost productivity to higher levels of return? Unfortunately, as appealing as they seem on the surface, these types of ratios are usually too simple to assess the details of productivity contributed by new communication media. However, they are a useful overall index. They also illustrate how technology can be a substitute of capital investment for labor, or "capital-labor trade-off."

Capital-labor trade-offs obviously raise the social considerations of worker displacement, a political issue dating back to the nineteenth-century Luddites, who demonstrated against worker displacement by destroying textile manufacturing machinery. Abstractly, one can look at capital-labor trade-offs both positively and negatively. On the positive side, one can argue that new communication systems can make existing workers more productive, hence creating growth for the company and new opportunities for worker advancement. But on the negative side a technology investment may allow a company to accomplish the same amount of work with fewer workers paid at no higher, or perhaps lower, rate than the original work crew. Lower wages for the workers may result if the technology allows for "deskilling"—that is, a lessening of the worker skills necessary to perform the tasks (e.g., many data-entry systems are increasingly designed to be operated by minimum-wage, unskilled personnel).

These social and political considerations, although unfortunately not a basic component in productivity calculations, may need to be considered in any practical analysis. For example, will the costs of worker relocation or retraining be included in the costs of technology implementation?

RETURN-ON-INVESTMENT RATIOS

We should also note that the efficiency formula is often used when the productivity of a business is assessed in terms of return on investment (or equity). Suppose, for example, in terms of expenses for labor, management, overhead, and supplies, a business returns $1.20 for every dollar of costs—a return of 20 percent. If costs are unchanged and the return is increased to $1.35, that is a 35 percent return, a difference of 15 percent. New communication investments can be considered in this type of analysis as their capital and operating costs are added to the equation. In a more detailed analysis, technology costs can be "factored" and examined relative to gains or losses. An example of this type of research is included under the later discussion of value-added analyses.

Finally, although our examples have a business environment, similar analyses of productivity as efficiency can be applied to nonprofit organizations. Public schools, for example, often describe their operating costs relative to enrollment, as in "$3,567 per student." This figure can be factored into overhead, management costs, technology costs, or bond indebtedness.

RATIOS RELATIVE TO VALUE ADDED

Still another strategy for evaluating technology impacts is to calculate a ratio of the cost of some level of operating expense (including technology) to an estimate of the value generated by different component investments in a business. The particular value generated is called value added. First, one can look at overall assessments of value added, and then see how technology investments fit into the picture.

Suppose, for example, that the total revenues of a business were $1 million. If the costs of raw materials and all expenses other than personnel (labor and management) for doing business were $800,000, the total value added would be $200,000. In other words, that is the value added to the raw materials (and nonpersonnel expenses) by the activities of individuals in the business. If the costs of personnel were $100,000, then the "personnel productivity" would be 2.0—that is, taking all other expenses into account, $1 in personnel creates $2 in total value added. Obviously, as personnel costs increase, and all other factors are held constant, the personnel productivity ratio would decrease, indicating that you got less for your increased investment in personnel.

Similarly, the productivity of labor or management can be described in a ratio to value added. Suppose labor costs were $75,000. This amount removed from the $200,000 total value added shows that $125,000 is the management value added. If the costs of management were $75,000, the management productivity ratio would be 1.67 (i.e., $125,100/$75,000).

Following this evaluation strategy, one could examine the costs of, say, computers relative to management value added as a productivity ratio. Suppose the cost of computers were $10,000; this amount relative to $125,000 is 12.5 as a ratio of technology productivity. However, this value is not altogether meaningful unless compared with some alternative. For example, computer systems of different capacities and costs could be compared to see if the greater capacity computer increased labor productivity.

More on the Value-Added Concept

Value added can also be examined in many detailed forms. For example, an improvement in the efficiency of transaction processing may have a simple effect of decreasing the costs of that processing. But it may have greater value relative to such effects on the business as improving cash flow, lowering interest costs, or improving competitive position. These latter values fit the concept of value-added analyses. In a business, these values almost always relate to profitability or the value of the business itself. In a nonprofit organization, these values may relate to the cost of providing services.

A value-added assessment can gauge the effect of technology investments in economic terms. As with traditional value-added analyses, the rationale is to calculate the contribution of the operation in terms of taking raw materials and operational costs to create a product or service that has enhanced value. The value may be assigned by what the market will return in the monetary amount of sales or increased valuation of the company. (This, however, would overlook such positive factors as increased customer loyalty or employee satisfaction until they contributed to increased revenues, company value, or lower costs). This return can then be assessed relative to capital investments, labor or managerial costs, or technology implementation. For new communication media, the assessment can be specifically focused on substitutions of technology for labor, enhanced management capabilities, or the value of newly gained information in general. An example of the latter might be the use of on-line market information services, where a company could better anticipate the demand for certain of its products and gear production accordingly.

Table 10–1 summarizes an example of productivity comparisons given by Paul Strassmann in *Information Payoff* (1985, p. 269). The technology investment is in office automation and the analysis covered three years. Note that the productivity change is positive when comparing 1980 (first column) with 1979, and 1979 with 1978. But this positive example should not overshadow the fact that productivity often decreases after initial investments in technology. As in the example of the on-line cataloging service in Chapter 9, the shakedown of the system contributed to rises in costs relative to benefits in the first year. Further, one needs to be cautious about the sources of effects when doing value-added analyses of technology investments. There are many subjective and difficult-to-quantify factors that may affect technology adoption—for example, managerial style, worker attitudes, quality of training to name a few. In all, value-added analyses may not be as detailed and precise as appears on the surface. Common sense and a detailed knowledge of the business or organization are especially valuable in these analyses.

As in the value-added example in the previous section, management value added is the monetary amount remaining after all costs except those for management are removed from total revenues. Management productivity could be calculated as a ratio of these values relative to management costs. Or, as in Table 10–1, technology pro-

Table 10–1. A Simplified Example of Productivity Analyses

Components	Year		
	1980	*1979*	*1978*
OUTPUT (thousands):			
Management value added	$1,247	1,233	1,012
INPUT:			
Technology costs	9.4	9.8	8.5
Relative productivity of information technology	132.66	125.83	119.06
Productivity change:		+5.4%	+5.7%

SOURCE: P. Strassman, *Information Payoff: The Transformation of Work in the Electronic Age* (New York: The Free Press, 1985), p. 269. By permission of the publisher.

ductivity could be examined as technology costs relative to management value added. These figures are valuable only for comparisons, in this case annual changes. If all factors where considered similarly, this approach could be used to compare two companies or two different communication system investments.

Examples of Productivity Analyses

BASIC COST-BENEFIT ANALYSIS

As you can see from the previous discussion, productivity analyses can take several forms. If the focus is on new communication system investment or operation, then you will want to calculate a ratio of system costs relative to some other component. Let us continue with the simplified example used in the opening of this chapter.

Table 10–2 summarizes the options we described for installing a computer in a small manufacturing firm. For roughly the same costs ($50,000 annualized over five years) the owner considered implementing computer-based assistance in either accounting or manufacturing. Table 10–2 presents the problem in terms of the calculations one could undertake (a computerized spreadsheet is a valuable tool for this analysis).

Note in Table 10–2 that all analyses are conducted relative to estimated gross revenues of $1 million. The "base" condition defines the status quo—that is, no computer investment. Also note that the return on investment is $325,000. The table then compares the rela-

Table 10–2. Simplified Cost-Benefits Calculation for Computer Applications

	Base	Accounting	Manufacturing	Both
Revenue	1,000,000	1,000,000	1,000,000	1,000,000
Costs				
Manuf.	650,000	650,000	585,000	585,000
Account.	25,000	12,500	25,000	12,500
Computer	.00	10,000	10,000	20,000
Returns $	*******	327,500	380,000	382,500
%	.325	.328	.380	.383

tive return on investment if computerization is applied to the accounting operations as against manufacturing. Although accounting costs could be reduced 50 percent by this investment, the return on costs is improved by only .003 as compared with an improvement of .05 by the application to manufacturing. Bear in mind that this is a simplified example to illustrate overall differences in technology investment; we have collapsed detailed costs into the overall figure. In a realistic evaluation, one might break out detailed costs of training, facilities remodeling, furniture, special air-conditioning, employee incentives, and the like. Further, remember that costs might rise while the system is being implemented, and this, too, might be estimated.

VALUE ADDED

Table 10–3 is a spreadsheet for a simplified value-added analysis of technology productivity. Again, assume that many of the details (training, depreciation, environment, etc.) are subsumed in the overall figures. The analysis will proceed as follows:

1. You will need data for entry into all lines except those for calculations of value added (spreadsheet cells B4 and B8) and productivity (i.e., C66, C10, and C12). These are all your cost items. If you are using an electronic spreadsheet, these are data entry cells.

2. Enter calculation formulas. Value-added calculations are based

Table 10–3. Simplified Value-Added Analysis
for a New Technology

A. Item	B. Value	C. Cost/Productivity
(1) Total Revenues	$1,000,000	
(2) Less Purchases	$720,000	
(3) Less capital cost	$80,000	
(4) Personnel value added	$200,000	
(5) Total personnel costs		$100,000.00
(6) Personnel productivity		2.00
(7) Less labor costs	$75,000	
(8) Management value added	$125,000	
(9) Management costs		$75,000.00
(10) Management productivity		1.67
(11) Technology costs		$10,000.00
(12) Technology productivity		12.50

on costs successively removed from total revenues. Enter formulas into these cells. The formula for B4 is B1 − (B2 + B3); for B8, it is B4 − B7. Productivity ratios are costs relative to added value. Formulas are: C6 = B4/C5; C10 = B8/C9; C12 = B8/C11.

3. These analyses are only meaningful if comparisons are made. You could use the spreadsheet in Table 10–3 to compare several "What if?" calculations. For example, calculations might show that for every $100,000 increase in revenues, with all other factors being equal, technology productivity increases .10. Or for $10,000 increments in technology costs, with all other factors being equal, technology productivity would decrease as follows:

Costs	Productivity
$20,000	6.25
$30,000	4.17
$40,000	3.13

Such comparisons could be useful in analyzing or planning technology benefits for a business. You may find a usual range of productivity for a particular type of technology application. If you are below or above this range, it is a signal to make changes.

CAPITAL-LABOR TRADE-OFF

Table 10–4 illustrates a simplified capital-labor trade-off for a technology investment. Five workers each earning $50 a day are replaced by three workers and a computer, the latter costing $100 per day. Using a computer, the three workers can process 500 more transactions per day than did the five workers without such help. These calculations illustrate how this contrast can be examined in terms of various productivity ratios. Note that cost-effectiveness shows that for every $1, the worker-only team can process four transactions, whereas the computer-assisted counterpart can process six. There are no changes in overall costs of the processing. The gains come from computerization making the workers more efficient.

However, as discussed earlier, there is still the consideration of social and political ramifications of worker displacement. It may be important to consider costs of worker relocation, upgrades of job descriptions and wages, or contribution to growth of the business. Simply "externalizing" the personal and social costs of worker displacement in a productivity analysis may not only be shortsighted, it may also be an aspect of control and exploitation that has repercussions throughout society. A more socially aware analysis would consider how to retrain those two workers for productive employment elsewhere in the organization.

Table 10–4. Simplified Example
of Capital-Labor Trade-off

	Base	Computerized
INPUT:		
Labor cost	$250	150
Technology cost	0	100
OUTPUT:		
Transactions/day	1,000	1,500
RATIOS:		
Cost-effectiveness	4	6
Labor ratio	.25	.10
Technology ratio	0	.07
Increase:		1.47

New Media as Strategic Investment

SELECTING OPTIONS

Much of what we have concentrated on in this chapter focused on the premise that some communication investments are better than others. A key distinction is in the benefits, the productivity, or value added by the new system. The concept of technological contribution to the operation of a business or organization is provided by the model in Figure 10–1. This approach is used by the firm of Booz Allen and Hamilton to illustrate strategic options for new media investment. It focuses on how computers or telecommunications may affect the value-added stream of a typical business organization. This model can also be easily adapted for use with both business and public service organizations (e.g., health, education, government). It shows that for a business, we could examine enhancement of such value-added functions as market planning, engineering, sales, or the network interconnecting account management, administration, and transactions.

An important assumption of this model is that if the proper strategic investments are made in new communication media, the resulting productivity will give a business or organization a competitive advantage. Following is a well-known example.

GAINING COMPETITIVE ADVANTAGE

For a decade or two, until about 1980, computer-based systems were perceived by most U.S. executives as tools for administration and management support. Examples are computer word processing, electronic messaging systems, and teleconferencing. But in the early 1980s, several cases of business success showed that these media were also powerful means of gaining a competitive advantage over one's rivals. One of these was American Airlines, the company that pioneered a computerized reservation system called Sabre.

American Airlines has a long tradition as the most innovative airline in the United States. It was the first company to launch a frequent flyer program in 1981. The AAdvantage program gave awards ranging from a free upgrade to first class after 12,000 miles of

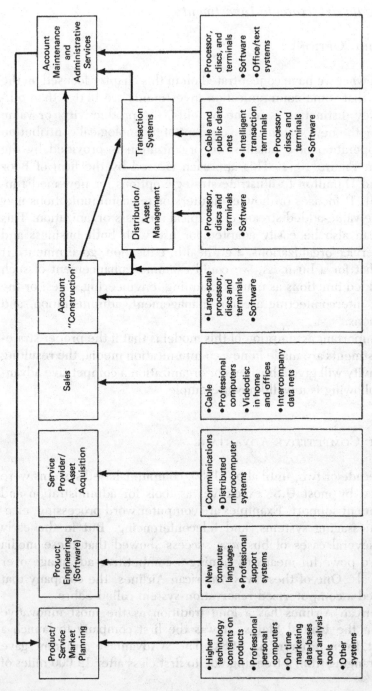

Figure 10–1. Potential Technological Impact on a Typical Services Value-Added Stream

SOURCE: Booz Allen and Hamilton, *Formulating IR Strategy for the 1980's.*

travel on American Airlines flights, to two free first-class tickets for 75,000 miles. This frequent flyer program was immediately copied by competitors; no airline could afford not to respond. At this point, AAdvantage looked like an effort to build customer loyalty to gain a short-term increase in market share, which would be limited in its competitive impact.

But there was much more to American's frequent flyer program because it was only one part of the company's general plan to use communication technology to gain an information edge. By 1981, American had spent seven years and $200 million on Sabre. Its computer reservations system allowed American to build a data-base on the 400,000 travelers who represent 70 percent of full-fare travel in the United States. The AAdvantage data on members' flights and their personal profiles were entered into the Sabre system. Then American could target commnication messages at particular customer segments. For example, say that a Mary Anderson is sitting in seat 4A on an American flight. The Sabre system communicates through a computer terminal in the cockpit to alert the flight attendants that Ms. Anderson is an AAdvantage Gold Card holder—a super-frequent flier—and hence worthy of special attention. Ms. Anderson's awareness of how the American computer system can track her personal characteristics occurs just after takeoff when the stewardess tells her: "Ms. Anderson, here is your favorite drink, compliments of the American Sabre System." Sabre knows that Ms. Anderson prefers orange juice on a morning flight and vodka tonic in the afternoon. Later, Ms. Anderson will receive a special mailing about American flights to Miami and San Diego, as Sabre also knows that she likes ocean cruises.

By 1986, American's Sabre system had captured 40 percent of the travel agent computerized reservations business in the United States. United's Apollo system followed with 31 percent of the market; Delta, TWA, and Eastern shared most of the rest. None of American's competitors, however, was prepared in 1981 to cope with the combination of AAdvantage and Sabre. For example, one airline asked its frequent flyers to write in their flight numbers on a card, which was not machine-readable. So the airline had to hire additional employees to enter these data in its computer system. Even then, the airline could not link the frequent flyer data with its computer reservations system.

Meanwhile, American was using its data-base to schedule its flights to maximize its load factor (the percentage of a plane's seats that are filled). Much too late, American's competitors realized that its computerized reservations and the AAdvantage program provided American with a precious data-base of customer information. In an industry where the potential value of an unsold passenger seat is lost forever, such information is of considerable competitive advantage.

Summary

There are many levels of cost analysis that go beyond cost-benefits. In the largest sense, it's whether new communication investments contribute to the overall effectiveness of a business or organization. Often, alternatives for technology applications, although attractive at a cost-benefits level, may have different effects upon the overall business, as was described at the top of this chapter in the example of accounting versus manufacturing control applications of computing.

The basic formula of "efficiency = input/output" can be examined on many levels, ranging from an individual technology investment to the performance of an overall business. Variations of this basic formula are: ratios of revenues relative to personnel or technology costs, return on investment ratios, and ratios relative to value added. The concept of value added is especially useful in identifying opportunities for communication technology investment in a business. Several examples were given for value-added analysis of computer investments.

In a much larger perspective, one can examine how productivity investments add to a company's competitive advantage, as in the example of American Airlines' reservation services.

PART III

New Considerations

CHAPTER 11

New Theoretical Approaches

The Need for New Theory

While the preceding chapters discussed a variety of methods that are appropriate for the study of the new media, such methods are misleading unless applied in the context of relevant theory. Many new media are the product of the convergence of computers and telecommunications networks (Chapter 1). Computers increase the interactivity of communication media; telecommunications networks increase the possibilities for communication among individuals or other units. Individuals, groups, and institutions can overcome the constraints of time, space, and interactivity inherent in conventional mass media to develop extended, new relationships (Rice, 1987b). Thus, theories that emphasize communication networks and interaction are particularly appropriate for the study of new media. Here we explore two theoretical approaches for understanding the implications of new media for networks and interactivity: relational convergence as a function of human communication networks, and involvement as a function of interactivity. These two examples show how appropriate theories and methods can be integrated in studies of the new media.

The Networks and New Media

NETWORK PARADIGM, DATA, MEASURES, AND METHODS

Communication can be seen as an interactive process of convergence rather than as a linear transmission of a message from a source to a receiver through a fixed channel. The patterning of these interactions and the process of convergence can be conceptualized, measured, and analyzed as communication networks. A *network* is a patterned set of relations among a system of nodes.

The network paradigm refocused researchers' preoccupations with individuals as independent senders and receivers of messages toward a concept of individuals as nodes in a network of interdependent relationships. Instead of analyzing average values of aggregated individual-level variables, network analysis focuses on patterns of relationships among individuals. So the network approach is relational, instead of individualistic. The network paradigm requires different levels of analysis, and different properties of communication, than does a one-way linear model of communication. Human communication is a joint product of interactive relationships among the members of a system. Thus, networks are a natural focus for the study of the new media.

The basic data-set in network analysis is a matrix in which the value in cell (i,j) shows the intensity of the link from node i to node j (of a possible N nodes). *Intensity* is the strength of a relationship between two nodes in a network. Intensity can be measured by the presence or absence, strength, frequency, importance, liking, influence, and so on of a relationship between two nodes in a network. Nodes can be individuals, groups, organizations, industries, countries, and so on. They can also be individuals who attend a set of common events, unions that represent workers in the same businesses, and so on. The intensity of the link to node j reported by node i may not be equal to the intensity of the link to node i reported by node j if the relationship is actually not equal, is not reported as equal, or is an indicator of a directed relationship (such as superior-subordinate communication). Figure 11–1 provides an example of a who-to-whom network matrix, which can be used to calculate such network measures as:

1. The average number of linkages sent and received by a node, indicating the extent to which the node is a target and/or a source of communication
2. Individual-level measures of network structure, such as a node's connectedness, centrality, or reachability with respect to the other nodes in the network
3. Reciprocity and strength of dyadic relationships, where unequal exchanges may indicate hierarchical status relations or constraints on two-way communication

		Position 1	Position 2	Position 3	Position 4
	1	- 1 1 1 1 1 1	0 0 1 1 0 0	0 0 1 1 1 0 0	0 0 0 0
	2	1 - 0 1 0 0 1	0 0 1 1 1 0	1 0 0 0 1 1 0	1 0 0 0
Position 1	3	0 0 - 0 0 0 0	0 0 0 0 1 1	0 0 0 0 1 0 0	1 1 0 1
(seven	4	1 1 1 - 1 1 1	1 1 1 1 1 1	1 1 0 1 1 1 1	1 1 0 1
doctors)	5	1 1 1 1 - 1 1	1 1 1 1 1 1	1 1 1 1 1 1 1	1 1 1 1
	6	1 0 0 1 1 - 1	1 0 1 1 1 1	1 0 1 1 1 1 1	1 1 0 1
	7	1 1 1 1 1 1 -	1 1 1 1 1 1	1 1 1 1 1 1 1	1 1 1 1
	8	0 1 0 1 1 1 1	- 0 1 1 1 1	0 1 1 1 1 1 1	1 0 1 0
Position 2	9	1 1 1 1 1 1 1	1 - 1 1 1 1	1 1 1 1 1 1 1	1 1 1 1
(six	10	1 1 1 1 1 1 1	1 1 - 1 1 1	1 1 1 1 1 1 1	1 1 1 1
doctors)	11	1 1 1 1 1 1 1	1 1 1 - 1 1	1 1 1 1 1 1 1	1 1 1 1
	12	0 1 1 1 1 1 1	0 1 0 1 - 1	1 0 0 1 1 0 0	1 0 0 0
	13	1 0 1 1 1 0 0	0 0 0 0 0 -	0 1 0 0 1 0 1	0 1 0 1
	14	0 0 0 0 0 0 0	1 0 0 0 0 0	- 0 0 0 0 0 0	0 0 0 0
	15	1 0 0 0 0 0 0	1 0 0 0 0 0	0 - 0 0 1 0 0	0 0 0 0
Position 3	16	0 0 0 0 0 0 0	0 0 0 0 0 0	0 0 - 0 0 0 0	0 0 0 0
(seven	17	1 1 1 1 1 0 1	1 0 0 0 1 0	0 0 0 - 1 0 0	0 1 0 0
doctors)	18	0 0 1 1 1 0 0	0 0 0 0 1 0	1 0 0 0 - 0 0	1 0 0 0
	19	1 0 0 0 1 1 0	0 0 0 0 0 0	1 0 0 0 0 - 0	0 0 0 0
	20	1 0 0 0 0 0 1	1 0 0 0 1 0	0 0 0 0 0 0 -	0 0 0 0
Position 4	21	0 0 0 1 0 1 0	0 0 0 0 0 0	0 0 0 0 1 0 0	- 0 0 0
(four	22	1 0 1 1 0 1 0	1 0 0 0 0 0	1 0 0 1 0 0 1	0 - 0 0
doctors)	23	0 0 0 0 0 0 0	1 0 0 0 0 0	0 0 0 0 0 0 0	0 0 - 0
	24	1 0 0 0 0 0 1	0 0 0 0 0 0	0 0 0 0 0 0 0	1 0 0 -

Figure 11–1. A Network Matrix Showing Which of Twenty-four Physicians Reported That They Hold Discussions with Each of the Twenty-three Other Physicians in a Private Group Practice

Note: A "-" is in cell (i,i) (the diagonal) because network analysis typically does not consider discussions that physicians have with themselves to be a "relationship." A "1" in cell (i,j) indicates that the physician in row i reported having discussions with physician j. A "0" indicates no reported discussion. This binary value (presence = 1, absence = 0) is the simplest measure of the intensity of a relationship between two physicians. Note that two physicians may disagree as to whether they had discussions with each other. In that case, cell (i,j) has a value of "1" while cell (j,i) has a value of "0," or vice-versa. The matrix has been arranged to show the discussion relations within and between each of the four "positions" of physicians. Each position consists of the doctors identified as having similar network relations by the network analysis program CONCOR.

Source: Adapted from Anderson and Jay (1985).

4. Intransitivity of triadic relationships, which may indicate the presence of "weak ties" in a network, allowing the transmission of new, innovative, and diverse information (Granovetter, 1982) (Note: Intransitivity occurs when node A communicates with node B, and node B communicates with node C, but A and C do not communicate.)

5. Membership in clusters or cliques, which distinguishes participants from isolates or similar nodes from dissimilar nodes
6. Relationships among cliques in the network, which may indicate patterns of intraorganizational coordination and integration or interorganizational imbalances in exchanges of resources
7. The distribution of network roles in cliques and in the total network, such as liaisons, opinion leaders, boundary-spanners, and isolates

A wide variety of methods for analyzing communication networks has been developed, spurred by the application of computers for handling the large number of network relations possible in even a moderately sized group (Knoke & Kuklinski, 1982; Rice & Richards, 1985; Rogers & Kincaid, 1981). For instance, 276 network links are possible among the twenty-four physicians in Figure 11-1 (24 × 23/2).

There are two basic approaches to conceptualizing and identifying the ways in which nodes in a network can be categorized. Both approaches have been applied to analyzing the adoption of innovations in general and to the adoption and use of the new media (Burt, 1987; Rice, 1982).

The "cohesion" approach argues that individuals reduce their uncertainty about an innovation by talking with, and learning the experiences of, those individuals who have already adopted. A network group (or clique) is a set of individuals (or other types of nodes) who have cohesive (dense, strong, frequent) relationships with each other but not with individuals outside their group. The "positional" approach argues that how individuals share positions in a social system influences the members' behavior and attitudes. A network position is a set of individuals (or other types of nodes) who have similar patterns of relationships with other individuals in the network, but do not necessarily have relationships with individuals within the position.

Influence of Networks on Adoption of Computer Systems

Researchers have investigated networks both as a dependent variable measuring the development of communication relationships within or across new media (Chapter 6 provides many examples) and as an independent variable measuring patterns of influence on the adoption of new media. The following section discusses this latter concern.

Adoption of computer-based health information systems by physicians in the United States has been, in general, much slower than expected. Anderson and Jay (1985), as well as other researchers, attempted to understand the social contexts, interaction patterns, and professional interpretations of the new computerized information systems that influence this unexpected reluctance to adopt. Anderson and Jay used network analysis to understand why some of the twenty-four physicians in a private group practice located next to a hospital used a computer-based hospital information system more than other physicians in the group practice did. The computer system allowed physicians and nurses to enter, access, change, and delete patients' records at terminals located in the hospital.

Anderson and Jay asked the twenty-four physicians to indicate which of the other physicians they referred patients to, held consultations about patients with, had discussions of professional matters with, and took calls for. Data about each of these four types of network relationships (referrals, on-call coverage, discussions, and consultations) were entered into separate twenty-four-by-twenty-four matrices, with a "1" if the communications relationship existed and a "0" if it did not. Figure 11–1 shows the who-to-whom matrix for the "discussion" relation.

Using the combination of all four matrices, a network analysis program called CONCOR identified four positions of physicians whose patterns of relationships (their columns in the matrix) were highly correlated with the patterns (columns) of other physicians. Physicians in *different* positions had columns that were not correlated. For example, as Table 11–1 shows, physicians in positions 1 and 2 generally had discussions with physicians in all other positions, but those in positions 3 and 4 did not, in general, report having discussions with physicians in any other position, including their own. These results from a positional approach are clearly different from the results of a cohesion approach, which would categorize the respondents into groups of physicians who had more discussions with each other than with physicians in other groups.

The authors also collected computer-monitored data on the usage of the system by each of the doctors during a six-day period. These data were merged with demographic and attitudinal data gathered by questionnaire. As Table 11–1 shows, the questionnaire data indicated that physicians in positions 1 and 2 were older and more active in

Table 11-1. Density, Network Relations, Age, and Percentage
Use of a Computer Information System for Four Network Positions
of Twenty-four Physicians in a Private Group Practice

	Position 1	Position 2	Position 3	Position 4
Density of Relations:				
Position 1	74%	71%	67%	64%
Position 2	86	73	79	71
Position 3	31	17	10	7
Position 4	29	8	14	8
Multiple Network				
Relations:	55%	39%	32%	23%
Average Age:	52 yrs.	44 yrs.	45 yrs.	39 yrs.
Computer Use:	45%	25%	20%	00%

The density figures are derived from Figure 11-1.
Density of relations is the percentage of all discussion relationships that were reported within or between each position.
Multiple relations is the percentage of physicians in a given position that reported more than one of the four possible relationships (referred patients, consulted, discussed professional matters, took calls) with the other physicians.
Computer use is the percent of each physician's medical orders that were entered directly through a terminal over a sample period of six days.
SOURCE: Adapted from Anderson and Jay (1985).

professional medical activities, and their use of the computer-based information system was greater than that of physicians in positions 3 and 4.

Anderson and Jay's (1985) analysis showed that network position was more strongly correlated with earlier adoption of, and greater use of, the hospital information system than any other variable in their study. Theories of social modeling, of social stratification, and of network position helped explain adoption and use of the hospital computer information system. The positions of the physicians in professional networks were a better explanation of adoption and use than either measures of cohesion (direct professional relationships) or demographic variables characterizing the physicians. For example, note that four doctors in position 4 did not use the computer information system at all (Table 11-1). These four individuals were almost isolates in the network, and represented an isolate professional position. In contrast, the seven physicians in position 1, who all had similar patterns of discussions with most of the physicians in the practice, used the computer information system the most.

In the theoretical context of understanding how communication relationships are associated with the adoption, use, and structuring of new media, network analysis is a particularly appropriate method to use in the study of new media.

Interaction and Involvement

THE NATURE OF INTERACTIVITY

One of the unique characteristics of many new media is their greater interactivity compared to the conventional mass media (Chapter 1). This greater interactivity in mediated human communication provides an appropriate setting for developing and testing theories of involvement.

"Involvement" is defined and operationalized in many ways. Broadly, it refers to the degree to which an individual actively participates in an information-exchange process. Involvement may be *psychological*, through perceptual and cognitive processes that are either involuntary, such as seeing visual images from an interactive videodisc, or voluntary, such as interpreting the meaning of these images to decide which frame to select next. Involvement also can be *social*—that is, being involved with other individuals by interacting with them, perhaps through a communication medium. These two levels (psychological and social) may interact, as in computer conferencing where the relationships among group members may set norms that influence what kinds of messages are read and what kinds are ignored.

How is interactivity in the new media—due to the form of messages or characteristics of the media—associated with psychological or social involvement? This question is not new: McLuhan (1964) categorized media as "hot" or "cool" depending on their level of ambiguity or the degree of information processing that they required from the user. Krugman (1965) suggested that the extent to which an individual made connections (a conscious bridging of the medium's message with one's experiences or personal references) is greatly influenced by characteristics of the medium. Both McLuhan and Krugman felt that television, for example, is a "cool" medium because it does not generally require much involvement by the viewer. This low involvement is one explanation for the susceptibility of television audiences to entertaining, repetitive messages about low-salience products and issues.

PSYCHOLOGICAL INVOLVEMENT AND INTERACTIVE VIDEODISCS

The concept of psychological involvement has generated two main controversies: (1) the ways in which involvement is conceptualized, and (2) the process by which it influences knowledge, attitudes, and behavior.

Involvement has been conceptualized in several ways: a personality trait, indicated by motivation; an internal state, indicated by levels of attention; dependency on the salience of the stimulus, leading to cognitive information processing; and a property of the stimulus, such as characteristics of the message or of the communication medium (Chaffee & Roser, 1986; Salmon, 1986).

Roser (1987) concluded that psychological involvement has two primary components: the cognitive component of paying *attention* to the message, and the affective component of *salience* of the message. Her research results showed that attention was important and sufficient in explaining increases in knowledge about a heart disease prevention campaign, but that involvement was necessary to explain changes in the audience members' attitudes and behaviors. Extending these results to the new media, a message available from a graphics teletext service may generate high attention (as a result of color and graphics on a terminal screen) but not much salience (Champness & deAlberdi, 1981). Or, information may have great salience but not draw much attention, such as videotext information about health or financial issues (Dozier & Rice, 1984).

Several models of the theoretical relationship among the concepts of involvement, knowledge, attitudes, and behavior have appeared in recent years (Roser, 1987; Salmon, 1986). One model posits these relationships as a psychological or social judgment process. Here if an individual is highly involved in the topic (that is, personally ego-involved), favorable messages lead to greater attitude change while unfavorable messages lead to greater resistance to attitude change. In other words, involvement leads to attention to, and processing of, the substance of the knowledge (in the form of the *strength* of the arguments). And this further leads either to (1) positive changes in attitude (and possibly behavior), or (2) increases in counterarguing behavior and greater resistance to change. This sequence is referred to as the "central route" of persuasion (Petty & Cacioppo, 1984).

However, if an individual is not much involved in a communication behavior, the more superficial aspects of the message and medium—such as the *number, cues,* or *source credibility* of the arguments—may affect attitudes but probably not behavior. Further, low involvement allows distractions (that may be part of the situation, the message, or the medium) to inhibit counterarguing, also leading to greater persuasion. Note that this "peripheral route" short-circuits the hypothesized process of persuasion that operates through a hierarchy of effects, passing sequentially through exposure, attention, processing, recall, persuasion, and behavior (McGuire, 1981). Only when involvement is high, and information is accessible, does knowledge lead to attitude change (a reasoned product of knowledge) and subsequent behavior. Otherwise, messages may lead to changes in knowledge and possibly behavior without changes in attitude. Or behavior may result from highly salient messages, followed by attitude changes to reduce dissonance and possible information-seeking (Chaffee & Roser, 1986).

One example of research investigating the role of interactivity in psychological involvement is the use of an interactive videodisc to provide information to significant others (such as family members) of cancer patients (Van Tassel, 1987). Computers can be programmed to present combinations of text, graphics, sound, and full-motion video information that is stored optically on a videodisc. These combinations can be preprogrammed by the system designer or selected interactively by the user. In this research, the computer was programmed to provide four decreasing levels of interactivity. Subjects who experienced the first two levels could respond by touching parts of the screen that were associated with multiple-choice answers to questions or prompts shown on the video screen. The four levels of interactivity were:

1. High: Users self-disclose emotions by providing affective reactions to the material as it is presented.
2. Medium: Users identify what emotions are projected by the material as it is presented.
3. Low: Users can choose to review portions of the material.
4. None: Users simply view a videotape of the same material.

The subjects answered a questionnaire before and after their session with the videodisc or videotape.

The theoretical argument was that active interaction with the choice, pacing, and evaluation of the content will require or induce greater cognition and motivation. This involvement should lead to different levels of learning (recall, comprehension, and processing activity), attitudes (mood and long-term emotional response to the patient), or behavior (intentions toward communication with the patient and estimated persistence in providing support for the patient).

The results of this exploratory study showed only one significant, systematic difference between users in the interactive group versus the noninteractive groups. Those in the noninteractive conditions correctly answered more cognitive questions about cancer and its treatment than did those subjects in the interactive groups.

Interactivity showed no other direct effects on users. However, high-level interactivity did evoke significantly higher levels of involvement. Users who were highly involved in their attitudes toward the presentation differed from those low in involvement. Highly involved subjects liked the presentation significantly better and estimated that it was more relevant.

Further, subjects who experienced higher levels of involvement while watching the presentation indicated that they would communicate more with the cancer patient, and more with others besides the cancer patient, than those subjects who had lower levels of involvement. Not only did highly involved subjects say they would talk more, they also reported differences in the content of what they would say to the patient. For example, while almost all the highly involved users reported that they would advise the cancer patient to comply with the doctor's course of treatment, only slightly more than half of those with lower involvement indicated that they would urge such compliance.

A major operationalization problem in this study was to produce the video, text, and audio materials and assemble them into videodisc format, and then develop the on-screen, interactive questions that initiated users' responses. Formative evaluation (Chapter 8) played an important role here. A major methodological data collection problem was to capture data about both the on-screen prompts as well as the subjects' responses, and to convert these data into a form that could be statistically analyzed. The analytical challenge was to conceptualize how different patterns of question-and-response could be jointly analyzed in the context of the theoretical model of interactivity, involvement, and outcomes. These issues are even more complex than some of the problems in managing computer-monitored data from computer communication systems (Chapter 6). This and similar studies may advance our understanding of the concepts of psychological involvement and new media interactivity.

SOCIAL INVOLVEMENT AND PARASOCIAL INTERACTION

Another related body of research concerns the form and influence of "parasocial interaction," the "interpersonal involvement of the media user with what he or she consumes" (Rubin et al., 1985, p. 156). This form of involvement with media personalities and content is theoretically similar in certain respects to interpersonal communication. It implies a kind of mutual control between audience members and media performers. The concept of parasocial interaction was originally proposed by Horton and Wohl (1956) in the context of performers on radio, television, and in the movies. The degree of parasocial interaction can be measured by the extent to which viewers or listeners: believe they know a performer, change their personal schedules to have a regular relationship through the medium with a performer, perceive a media personality as a friend, talk to performers while viewing or listening to the medium, look to the media personality for guidance, and try to contact directly the media performer.

A program can increase the perceived parasocial interaction of audience members by producing a show live, or having it appear to be live; blurring the boundaries between the in-studio program audiences and the home audiences; creating realistic and useful content; using production techniques such as zoom, close-up, and natural settings (including showing the production context itself); and maintaining continuity and context across media programs.

Thus, a wide variety of characteristics of the message and of the medium, along with individual perceptions and situations, contribute to parasocial interaction. Social and psychological forces such as media dependency (Ball-Rokeach et al., 1984), ritualistic or instrumental use of the media (Dozier & Rice, 1984), and certain demographics (older age, lower education and income) also increase the degree of perceived parasocial interaction. Past research shows that parasocial interaction is an additional type of communication interaction and is not related to loneliness or to levels of consumption of the medium. However, parasocial interaction does influence expectations that lead to further media use (Rubin et al., 1985).

To what extent is parasocial interaction perceived through the new media? How is this process associated with new social forms of communication, distortion, or inequities? For example, Beniger (1987) sees a blurring of interpersonal and mass communication into what he calls "pseudo-communities" because of increasingly diverse ways in which the mass media are personalized, and in which they increase perceptions of parasocial interaction. For example, political campaigns increasingly use data-bases that combine public records of whether individuals voted or not, and their party affiliation, with direct-mail lists for mass mailings of customized, laser-printed letters to solicit contributions or advocate support for a political candidate or a referendum issue. Because computers can be used to design the content and appearance of mass-produced letters (including a realistic signature by the candidate) based on information about residents within particular zip codes and their past voting behavior, a reader may perceive the letter to be a personal appeal based on some level of familiar interaction. The problem, Beniger (1987) argues, is that there is no *true* interaction or interactivity, so there is no way for the audience to judge, assess, or inspect the integrity of the source, content, or medium. Further, an unintended infrastructure of pseudo-community may arise that is really the product of a small group of media elites who control the production and distribution of these messages.

What are the methodological implications of studying parasocial involvement and pseudo-communities? One is the need to develop measures of both actual and perceived interactivity of computer-modified media such as telemarketing, direct mail, or dating conferences on bulletin boards. The second implication is to use research methods such as questionnaires, focus groups, and participant observation to understand whether users perceive greater parasocial interaction in these computer-modified media than in their unmodified form. Interpretive approaches seem to be appropriate ways to understand the form and consequences of the possible new realities of parasocial interaction and pseudo-communities. Finally, long-term sociological analyses of social control and of special interest groups can help improve our understanding of the implications of the new media for the hypothesized development of pseudo-communities of new media users.

Summary

Communication theories of network processes, and of interactivity and involvement, can expand our understanding of how individuals communite *with* the new media, as well as how they communicate *about* the new media.

One appropriate theoretical and methodological framework for studying the new media is a model of communication as a process of relational convergence. This convergence may be the process by which other theoretical frameworks—such as social stratification, social influence, or the diffusion of innovations—can be applied to the study of the new media. Networks can be conceptualized as both the social structure and the individual relationships that influence the adoption of new media, as well as the form in which use of these new media is manifested. In network analysis, the communication relationship is the unit of analysis. It can be analyzed at a variety of levels. The new media are uniquely able to provide data about network relationships among users.

Another potentially powerful theoretical approach to understanding better the new media combines theories of psychological and social involvement with the concept of interactivity of the new media. Because the new media provide for, and often require, greater levels of interactivity than do traditional mass media, an individual's involvement with their content is generally expected to be greater. However, this increased involvement may be based on misleading parasocial signals about the integrity and reality of media content.

CHAPTER 12

Issues of Ethics and Ideology

Human Costs and Benefits

Conforming to certain moral and social standards should not be a new topic to the communications researcher, yet there are topics associated with new media that have powerful ethical implications of which there are two types: those seen as special responsibilities of researchers in their work with human subjects and new media, and ethical issues associated with the growth and uses of the new communication media.

Standards for research with human subjects is dictated by Federal Regulation in the United States. Researchers encounter this Regulation in the standards required by most federal or private agencies that support research, and especially by university review committees. Today, in most U.S. universities, any research project involving human beings may be subject to a conformance review. We examine these requirements in the first part of this chapter.

The second category of implications reflects concerns frequently raised in our times regarding uses, effects, and broad social implications of new communication media. Research activities often place priorities on certain types of growth, whether or not ethical implications are considered. For example, as discussed in Chapter 10, there are social implications to be considered when communication media are developed to replace human workers ("dislocation") or to lessen the requirements for their operation (i.e., "deskilling"). There is also the growing problem of privacy and access, especially when considering personal information stored in data-bases.

Finally, there is the question of equity in the distribution or availability of communication media in the society at large. For example, what are the costs of broadcast or telephone deregulation to society in terms of the availability and quality of services? How should journalists and editors change their professional standards to avoid the fragmentation of news content potentially associated with videotex newspapers? In a commercially and market-oriented communication technology economy, should researchers give special priority to fairness, quality, or equity studies? It is often argued that if they do not, there will be nobody promoting these concerns. A discussion of several selected privacy and equity issues makes up the second half of this chapter, while other discussions are available in a special issue of *Communications* (1986) on "Ethics and New Media."

Research with Human Subjects

BACKGROUND

Until the mid-1970s, a social science researcher was free to deal with human subjects in almost any way short of physically endangering them. (Medical research had specific guidelines.) Consequently, most of the landmark experiments in persuasion or media-based aggression carried out with college sophomores was conducted without any special review for the welfare of the human subjects. If a review were required of a researcher who went into the schools to gather data, it was usually requested by a local committee with their own standards. Now, some ten to fifteen years later, the pendulum has swung to the opposite side—not entirely, but enough so that most communication researchers who deal directly with human subjects, and who follow the rules, will see their research plans evaluated. For example, the American Psychological Association (1981) and researchers on computer-human interaction (Allen, 1984) have developed explicit codes of research ethics.

Part of the background for present standards comes from the National Research Act (Public Law 93–348), which was passed in 1974. The main charge of the act was to define the basic ethical principles that were to guide biomedical behavioral research involving human subjects. Activities involved the establishment of a special commission to develop guidelines for human subjects research. The report of this group, popularly known as the Belmont Report (*Federal Register*, 1979), remains influential today.

THE BELMONT REPORT

The Belmont Report duly acknowledges the many contributions of scientific research to humankind, but it also recognizes that human guinea pigs have been subjected to many abuses, especially in biomedical research. One benchmark for standards was the criteria used during the Nuremberg War Crimes Trials (Nuremberg Code) to judge the behaviors of physicians and scientists who conducted biomedical experiments on concentration camp inmates. The Belmont Report drew from these criteria as well as other "codes" developed in response to them. A main premise in the Report is the distinction between "practice" and "research."

For medical practices, there should be no motive for activities other than those presumed to benefit the patient. By contrast, research activities should be of the hypothesis-testing nature, permit scientific conclusions to be drawn, and the results should contribute to generalizable knowledge. In other words, what is done to a human subject might be considered somewhat differently if it qualifies as research. Even treatment that is unusual or radical may not be considered research unless it is in an investigatory paradigm. This boundary between research and practice is, of course, less directly relevant to communication researchers, but it is part of the background that gives the biomedical flavor to guidelines for research with human subjects.

The Belmont Report also states three basic ethical principles that we summarize briefly below. (Be aware that important details can be lost in a brief summary of this type.) The principles include:

1. *Respect for persons:* Humans should be treated as "autonomous agents" and given due respect for their attitudes, opinions, and behaviors. Humans of diminished capacity, as an ethical consideration, are entitled to protection.
2. *Beneficence:* There is an obligation to promote the well-being of human subjects, as in doing them no harm and in maximizing their benefits.

3. *Justice:* This is a response to the question: Who ought to receive the benefits of research and bear its burdens? An injustice is done when benefits are overlooked or denied, or when an undue burden is imposed. Are research subjects being selected simply because they are easily available (as with prison inmates, the poor, or students) rather than being specifically important to the research?

The Report concludes with specific suggestions for applying these principles. There are three guidelines, which are briefly summarized here:

1. *Informed consent:* To the extent possible, subjects should be given the choice of participation based on the knowledge of what may or may not happen to them.
2. *Assessment of risks and benefits:* There should be a systematic evaluation of any types of harm that may befall the subject as well as the potential benefits. Risks and benefits may typically apply to society as a whole as well as to the individual. Documentation of this assessment should be an important component for evaluation of a proposed project. Further, this information should be understandable to the subject in making the choice of whether to participate.
3. *Selection of subjects:* As in the discussion of "justice," subject selection should be guided by relevance to the research problem and not ease of availability. Particular care should be taken so as not to exploit "vulnerable" individuals, especially certain social, racial, sexual, or institutionalized groups.

Again, the Belmont Report is a major influence underlying Public Law 93-348 and the latter is enunciated through the Code of Federal Regulations 45 CFR 46, "Protection of Human Subjects," March 8, 1983. As a passing note, unlike many legal documents, the Belmont Report is remarkably clear and literate and makes for interesting reading.

INSTITUTIONAL GENERAL ASSURANCE

The "Institutional General Assurance" is a statement of compliance with federal regulations regarding research with human subjects. It is locally prepared by any institution associated with human subjects research, which includes virtually every university or university system. Among the requirements of the Assurance statement is that institutional review boards be established for the purpose of promoting and enforcing compliance with federal requirements. In most universities, this goes under the general title of the Committee for Research Involving Human Subjects. In larger institutions, there may be departmental or school-level review committees that screen projects at a preliminary level. It depends on how the individual institution has developed compliance with the Assurance statement.

Review committees are guided by the principles of the Belmont Report, but most institutional Assurance statements have further, specific criteria.

At the institutional level, review procedures vary, so it is important to study your institution's Assurance statement. In most interpretations, even if you are doing a personally directed study without outside support, you must follow your institution's guidelines if the research bears any relation to your professional responsibilities with the institution, it is done on their property, or it uses any type of institutional information or assistance for obtaining research subjects.

PRACTICAL NOTES

Being aware of your institution's human subjects committee and Assurance statement will prevent the major frustration of being ready to proceed with a study or with the submission of a grant application only to find that you must have your proposal reviewed. Reviews take time, and in the experience of at least one of the authors (F.W.), you may encounter the committees of medical or engineering researchers who are hostile to research outside of their mainstream, especially studies involving children.

All this may seem restrictive—and, in a sense, it is—but your institution's procedures may include many exceptions. For example, most survey or interview research may be exempt from review so long as it does not involve individuals in compromised situations or, in some cases, children. Also, research typically conducted in educational settings, as a part of normal educational activities, is often exempt from review. All such exemptions are a part of your institution's Assurance statement.

If your project is subject to review, there will be a locally prepared form to accompany your proposal. Also, you will likely need a synopsis of how your proposal conforms to human subjects guidelines. Figure 12–1 is an example of the synopsis required at the University of Texas.

Almost any research that involves human subjects in an experimental or quasi-experimental design requires a researcher to obtain a signed consent form from his subjects. An example of a consent form is given in Figure 12–2.

Privacy as an Example of an Ethical Issue

Making Private Information Public

The Tower Commission, which conducted one of the first investigations in 1987 of possible wrongdoing in the Iran-*contra* affair, found that the computer system used by Lt. Col. Oliver North had stored

---

Synopsis of Proposal: To Be Prepared and to Accompany Application for the Conduct of a Project Involving Human Subjects

1. Identify the sources of the potential subjects, derived materials, or data. Describe the characteristics of the subject population, such as their anticipated number, age, sex, ethnic background, and state of health. Identify the criteria for inclusion or exclusion. Explain the rationale for the use of special classes of subjects, such as fetuses, pregnant women, children, institutionalized mentally disabled, prisoners, or others, especially those whose ability to give voluntary informed consent may be in question.

2. Describe the recruitment and consent procedures to be followed, including the circumstances under which consent will be solicited and obtained, who will seek it, the nature of information to be provided to prospective subjects, and the methods of documenting consent. (Include applicable consent form[s] for review purposes.) If written consent is not to be obtained, specifically point this out and explain why not.

3. Describe any potential risks—physical, psychological, social, legal, or other—and assess their likelihood and seriousness. Describe alternative methods, if any, that were considered and why they will not be used.

4. Describe the procedures for protecting against or minimizing any potential risks and include an assessment of their likely effectiveness. Include a discussion of confidentiality safeguards, where relevant, and arrangements for providing medical treatment if needed.

5. Describe and assess the potential benefits to be gained by the subjects, as well as the benefits that may accrue to society in general as a result of the planned work.

6. Discuss the risks in relation to the anticipated benefits to the subjects and to society.

Figure 12–1. Human Subjects Proposal Synopsis

You are invited to participate in a study of *(state what is being studied).* We hope to learn *(state what the study is designed to discover or establish).* You were selected as a possible participant in this study because *(state why and how the subject was selected).* There will be *(number)* subjects in the study.

If you decide to participate, we (or: Dr. _____ and his associates) will *(Describe the procedures to be followed, including their purposes, how long they will take, and their frequency. Describe the discomforts and inconveniences reasonably to be expected, and any benefits reasonably to be expected).*

(Describe appropriate alternative procedures that might be advantageous to the subject, if any. Any standard treatment that is being withheld must be disclosed.)

Any information that is obtained in connection with this study and that can be identified with you will remain confidential and will be disclosed only with your permission. *(If you will be releasing information to anyone for any reason, you must state the persons or agencies to whom the information will be furnished, the nature of the information to be furnished, and the purpose of the disclosure.)*

Your decision whether or not to participate will not prejudice your future relations with the *(Institution or agency).* If you decide to participate, you are free to discontinue participation at any time without prejudice.

If you have any questions, please ask us. If you have any additional questions later, Dr. _____ *(give a phone number or address)* will be happy to answer them.

You will be offered a copy of this form to keep.

....

You are making a decision whether or not to participate. Your signature indicates that you have read the information provided above and have decided to participate. You may withdraw at any time without prejudice after signing this form should you choose to discontinue participation in this study.

_____   _____
Signature   Date

_____   _____
Signature of Parent or Legal Guardian   Date

(This line should not appear on
forms that will be given to subjects consenting themselves)

_____   _____
Signature of Witness (when appropriate)   Signature of Investigator

Figure 12–2. Example of a Subject Consent Form

all the messages exchanged between him and other members of the National Security Council (*Time*, 1987). Apparently, North, like many other users of electronic messaging systems, assumed that such messages were deleted automatically. They were, on his computer screen, but they were also transferred to a backup computer file for long-term storage. These "unobtrusive" data provided the Tower Commission with important insights into the secret (and possibly illegal) Iran-*contra* operations.

Similar data in all computer systems may be obtained by finding them on "backup" tapes that are regularly made to save files from accidental erasure, or by reconstructing the data in computer memory because only the file name, not the contents, is erased when a user "deletes" a file. Data also may be accessed through the original users' passwords, which are obtained either illegally or through careless security procedures.

A key event in breaking the Watergate case in the 1970s involved a computer record of certain long-distance telephone calls made by Donald Segretti of the Nixon White House staff. These calls concerned his task of laundering some "dirty money." Segretti had supposed that no record existed of these phone calls, but Bob Woodward and Carl Bernstein of the *Washington Post* were able to obtain a copy of Segretti's credit card calls from a computer data-base. In both of these examples, the possible invasion of privacy was legal and served positive purposes for society, but this legality may otherwise not be the case.

PERSONAL PRIVACY

A personal example of the consequences of perceived threats to privacy by consumers occurred when one of the authors of this book served as a "Sysop" (system operator) for his school's computer bulletin board system. Sysops have special privileges, such as access to a system's files to maintain the system. When the Sysop checked into the system to do some routine management duties, he was able to see that a student was currently entering a message into the computer bulletin board. Intending to be friendly, the Sysop sent a one-line welcoming comment directly to the user's screen. Convinced that his communication activities were being continuously monitored, the student never used the computer bulletin board again.

To many people, computers and data-bases represent the invasion of privacy by an increasingly technological world (Freedman, 1987; Turn, 1985; Westin & Baker, 1972). Data-banks now track our personal and professional lives, either directly or indirectly, either separately in one data-base or jointly through linked data-bases. Privacy problems are particularly encountered with financial data-bases. While privacy and data-protection laws in the United States and Europe have provided increasing protection to individuals, loopholes or ambiguous criteria for verifying or correcting information in data-bases can cause problems.

One recent U.S. survey found that between two-thirds and three-quarters of the public are genuinely concerned about issues of data privacy and accuracy, and their concerns are growing (Vidmar & Flaherty, 1985). Respondents in this study were even more concerned about protection of personal privacy than about nuclear war (which is consistently ranked as one of the most important problems facing U.S. society). A Texas survey found that 52 percent agreed or strongly agreed that "the government will be able to use new communication technology to invade people's privacy" (Reese et al., 1987). A comprehensive review of surveys concerning privacy and civil liberties found that the proportion of Americans "very" concerned about threats to their personal privacy grew from around 25 percent in 1974 to 48 percent in 1984. The proportion who believed that computer files were kept on them grew from 44 percent to 67 percent in the same decade, 84 percent believed it is easy to compile a master file on them, and 53 percent felt that computers are a threat to personal privacy. Respondents who were more liberal and had lower socioeconomic status were more concerned. Most respondents considered that the value of the new computer systems and services was a worthwhile trade-off for possible privacy concerns (Dutton & Meadow, 1987).

The quality, confidentiality, and security of information collected in computer data-bases are threatened in a growing number of ways. Automated services record information about our transactions (such as home banking through videotext services). Analysts can infer patterns of personal activities from the number and kinds of services used by an individual (such as the monthly charges listed on credit card records). Certain computer systems can be programmed to make automatic decisions about an individual based on a minimal set of data (such as processing a home loan application). Secondary markets exist for information collected about consumers in a primary market (such as credit reports sold to bankers based on a consumer's prior financial activities). Further, the consumer has less legal protection against private companies than against government agencies, which must follow federal regulations about collecting and releasing information. In the cable television industry, U.S. government regulations protect against the misuse of data collected through interactive cable systems. Extending earlier voluntary, municipal, or state regulations (e.g., Minnesota in 1980, Illinois in 1981, the Columbus, Ohio Qube system in 1981, and Wisconsin in 1982), Section 631 of the 1984 Communication Policy Act states that a cable operator can only collect data to obtain information necessary to render a cable service or other service, or to detect unauthorized reception. The public lacks awareness about what kinds of information are being collected in computer data-bases. And data can be integrated and matched across multiple data-bases (for example, cross-checking your auto driving record against your auto insurance company's files).

PROTECTING PRIVACY IN RESEARCH

Most individuals strongly resist the collection and analysis of the content of their messages in a new communication system. Knowing *who* an individual communicates with may be an even greater invasion of privacy. Most studies of computer networks have been explicitly experimental (Hiltz, 1982), public sponsored (Danowski, 1982), or government sponsored (Rice & Paisley, 1982). In such situations, individuals usually sign consent forms (giving the researcher permission to use such data) or voluntarily provide data about their who-to-whom communication networks. Other studies guarantee individual anonymity by randomly re-assigning respondent identification numbers to the data, so that the identity of specific individuals cannot be linked to specific data. Another solution is to gather and report only aggregate data (such as by region or by demographic category), so that no individual-level data are made available.

Equity as an Example of an Ethical Issue

New communication systems may provide benefits such as greater equality of participation, more innovative decision making, and fewer material, status, or social constraints on communicating with other individuals in a system. However, communities of new media users may also be more ephemeral, less empowered, more homogenized, and less socially cohesive than traditional personal and social networks (Rice, 1987a). Further, the potential benefits of decentralized access to information such as past experience of political candidates, product quality, or community health programs are simply not available to many individuals in society.

Even in rich, industrialized countries like the United States, many individuals and communities do not have economic or physical access to new communication technology, the training required to use such systems, or the educational background informing them of the value of some information. Specialized training (which is often highly related to socioeconomic status) may be necessary to become a user, technician, analyst, or manager of a computer-based system. Even if these constraints were removed, the typical user may not find, or be able to contribute, information of relevance to their particular needs and contexts. A key challenge for the communication researcher is to identify and document the variables that allow increased access to the powers of human interaction.

Although we have focused on the new media in this book, these issues of research with human subjects, privacy, and benefits are in no way limited to the latest communication media. They are a topic for all communication research as are many other important philosophical, social, and moral issues. Practitioners and researchers of all media must explicitly evaluate their definitions, values, principles, and loyalties when making decisions about content, systems, audiences, applications, and meanings (Christians et al., 1983). Because of computers and telecommunications networks, some media can be considered "new" at this time. Because of the rights and integrity of humans, ethics and privacy will continue to be complex and crucial issues for many years to come.

The new media, in many situations, have also been associated with negative, unintended, damaging, and/or politically divisive consequences. Issues of ethics, privacy, and individual rights have often been ignored (Mosco, 1982; Schiller, 1982; Slack & Fejes, 1984). Communication scholars should give greater attention to the identification, analysis, and prevention of such negative outcomes and explore how the new media may be part of a more ethical and liberating world. Researchers of new media should explore their theories, research designs, and methods to uncover assumptions about the new media that either ignore or even encourage such possible social conditions. Regardless of the method, design, or theoretical perspective used, communication researchers have a responsibility to focus on these issues. As Morgan (1983, p. 373) states succinctly:

> The pursuit of knowledge as but a particular form of human interaction . . . must be understood as being as much an ethical, moral, ideological, and political activity as it is an epistemological one.

Summary

Research involving the new media prompts several areas of ethical concern, including research with human subjects, rights to privacy, and equity in access to new media.

Although guidelines for use of human subjects in research are already known to most communication researchers, the interpretations have been modified in recent years. Moreover, technology applications—especially where one is assessing the manipulation of attitudes and behaviors—can raise ethical issues. Discussion in this section was focused on the Belmont Report, which set the standards for later guidelines involving human subjects research. Included in these guidelines are: (1) that research subjects be given due respect for their existing attitudes, opinions, and behaviors; (2) that there is an obligation to promote the well-being of subjects; and (3) that subjects should be selected because of relevance to, and benefits from, the research.

A major ethical issue in one area of new communication media, and one subject for research in itself, is that of privacy in an era of large public data-bases and the increasing capability of institutions to communicate among them. There is the issue, too, of protecting personal or organizational privacy in research, as when messages are recorded or observed from a private communications network.

The problem of equity has long been associated with communication media as in U.S. policies of "affordable" telephone service or broadcasting for "the public's interest, convenience, and necessity." Economic and educational stratification can easily be reinforced or even increased by unequal access to new media opportunities and experiences.

Ultimately, we must realize, and respond to, the fact that research with, and on, the new media has political, ideological, and ethical connotations.

On-line Data-base Services

This appendix lists a selection of the major on-line data-base services available at reasonable subscription rates for communication researchers or their institutions. Ask for educational discounts. Major guides to specialized data-bases include:

Databasics. New York: Garland Publishing Co.
Database Directory. White Plains, N.Y.: Knowledge Industry Publications, Inc.
Directory of Online Databases. Los Angeles: Cuadra Associates.
The Executive's Guide to Online Information Services. White Plains, N.Y.: Knowledge Industry Publications, Inc.

SELECTED DATA-BASE SERVICES

BRS/After Dark
    BRS/After Dark
    1200 Route 7
    Latham, NY 12100
    (800/833-4707)
    (800/553-5566 in New York state)
    (518/783-7251 from Alaska, Hawaii, and outside the United States)

The initials stand for Bibliographic Retrieval Service, and the After Dark refers to the fact that it offers low cost access to bibliographies during non–prime time hours on nights and weekends. BRS/After Dark offers an easily used system for on-line access to approximately eighty data-bases, including the sciences, medicine, business and finance, reference, education, social sciences, and humanities.

CompuServe
Consumer Information Service
5000 Arlington Centre Boulevard
P.O. Box 20212
Columbus, OH 43220
(800/848-8990)

CompuServe services include mail, conferencing, bulletin boards, direct communications, news, business items, programs, programming, educational information, and shopping. The service also offers a wide selection of interest groups and bulletin boards.

Dialog
Dialog Information Services
Marketing Department
3460 Hillview Avenue
Palo Alto, CA 94304
(800/227-1927)
(800/982-5838 in California)

Among the best of the professional-oriented data-base services is Dialog Information Services, Inc. It is considerably more expensive than such public-oriented services as The Source or CompuServe. A ten-minute search might run $10 to $15, but there are no start-up or subscription fees. (When inquiring, ask about their "Knowledge Index" service, a reduced-price option, or their Classroom Account, which provides considerable discounts to educational institutions.) Dialog's nearly 200 data-bases cover science, technology, chemistry, medicine, engineering, social sciences, business, economics, and current events. Dialog also offers regular training sessions for new users.

Dow Jones News/Retrieval
Dow Jones & Company, Inc.
P.O. Box 300
Princeton, NJ 08540
(800/257-5114)
(609/452-1511 in New Jersey)

Dow Jones News/Retrieval is operated by the publishers of the *Wall Street Journal* and *Barron's*, the longtime providers of market information. Its main offerings are business information, including files from its publications, but has been adding other items of interest. One of the most powerful features offered by Dow Jones News/Retrieval is their "text search." By using any combination of words, dates, or numbers, you can search through the Dow Jones files for anything published since June 1979. In addition to regular rates, you pay special fees for uses of certain data-bases.

Instant Yellow Page Service

Instant Yellow Page Service
5707 S. 86th Circle
P.O. Box 27347
Omaha, NE 68127
(402/331-7169)

You can access any of the over 4,800 *Yellow Page* telephone directories in this country from Instant Yellow Page Service, which is on-line twenty-four hours a day. You can gather data by region as well as business type and can even print address labels.

Nexis

Marketing Department
Mead Data Central
P.O. Box 1830
Dayton, OH 45401
(800/227-4908)

Nexis is the premier among services that offer retrieval from major periodicals, including the wire services and the *New York Times.* You can retrieve entire texts using a variety of search procedures including key words. Like the other professionally oriented services, Nexis is expensive. There is an initial fee for a terminal, a monthly subscription fee, plus hourly and surcharge costs, depending on how you use the service. Nexis also offers Lexis, an on-line retrieval service for legal information.

NewsNet

NewsNet
945 Haverford Road
Bryn Mawr, PA 19010
(800/345-1303)
(215/527-8030 in Pennsylvania)

Just about every specialized area of business is served by a professional newsletter, sometimes many of them. These newsletters are often expensive and are not easily found in traditional libraries. NewsNet is a service that currently offers access to nearly 200 business newsletters, in addition to United Press International and a special public relations newswire. You pay an hourly rate (currently $15), plus special surcharges that vary by newsletter.

Source (The)
   The Source Telecomputing Corporation
   1616 Anderson Road
   McLean, VA 22102
   (703/734-7500; 800/336-3366)

The Source is a subsidiary of The Reader's Digest Association, Inc. It offers services for communications, news, business, consumer information, entertainment, publishing, travel, education, and computing. One of the valuable features of The Source is access to the recent United Press International newswire files. Using a relatively simple command system, you can literally search the world's news for any specific topic. The Source's mail and bulletin board systems seem to enjoy wide use.

Tech Data
   Information Handling Services
   14 Inverness Way East
   Englewood, CO 80150
   (303/790-0600)

Tech Data is an engineering-oriented data-base service that includes industrial catalogs, standards, military and federal specifications, bibliographies, and other technologically oriented files.

References

ALBRECHT, T. L., AND V. A. ROPP. 1982. "The Study of Network Structuring in Organizations Through the Use of Method Triangulation." *Western Journal of Speech Communication* 46:162–178.

ALLEN, R. 1984. "Working Paper on Ethical Issues for Research on the Use of Computer Services and Interfaces." *SIGCHI Bulletin* 16(1):12–16.

AMERICAN PSYCHOLOGICAL ASSOCIATION. 1981. "Ethical Principles of Psychologists." *American Psychologist* 36(6):633–638.

ANDERSON, J. 1987. *Communication Research: Issues and Methods.* New York: McGraw-Hill.

ANDERSON, J., AND S. JAY. 1985. "Computers and Clinical Judgment: The Role of Physician Networks." *Social Science Medicine* 20(10): 969–979.

BABBIE, E. 1983. *The Practice of Social Research,* 3rd ed. Belmont, Calif.: Wadsworth.

BALES, R. 1950. *Interaction Process Analysis: A Method for the Study of Small Groups.* Reading, Mass.: Addison-Wesley.

BALL-ROKEACH, S. J., M. ROKEACH, AND J. W. GRUBE. 1984. *The Great American Values Test: Influencing Behavior and Belief Through Television.* New York: The Free Press.

BANTZ, C. 1983. "Naturalistic Research Traditions," in L. Putnam and M. Pacanowsky (eds.), *Communications and Organizations: An Interpretive Approach,* pp. 55–72. Beverly Hills, Calif.: Sage.

BASS, F. M. 1969. "A New Product Growth Model for Consumer Durables. *Management Science* 15:215–227.

BATESON, G. 1972. *Steps to an Ecology of Mind.* New York: Ballantine.

BENIGER, J. 1987. "Personalization of Mass Media and the Growth of Pseudo-Community." *Communication Research* 14(3):352–371.

BERGER, C., AND M. ROLOFF. 1980. "Social Cognition, Self-Awareness and Interpersonal Communications," in B. Dervin and M. J. Voigt (eds.), *Progress in Communication Sciences*, Vol. 2., pp. 2–49. Norwood, N.J.: Ablex.

BERNARD, H., P. KILLWORTH, D. KRONENFELD, AND L. SAILER. 1984. "The Problem of Informant Accuracy: The Validity of Retrospective Data." *Annual Review of Anthropology* 13:495–517.

BERNARD, H., P. KILLWORTH, AND L. SAILER. 1982. "Informant Accuracy in Social Network Data V." *Social Science Research* 11:30–66.

BONOMA, T. 1985. "Case Research in Marketing: Opportunities, Problems and a Process." *Journal of Marketing Research* 22:199–208.

BOYD, D., AND J. STRAUBHAAR. 1985. "Developmental Impact of the Home Videocassette Recorder on Third World Countries." *Journal of Broadcasting and Electronic Media* 29:5–21.

BRETZ, R. 1983. *Media for Interactive Communication*. Beverly Hills, Calif.: Sage.

BURRELL, G., AND G. MORGAN 1979. *Sociological Paradigms and Organizational Analysis*. London: Heinemann.

BURT, R. 1987. "Social Contagion and Innovation: Cohesion versus Structural Equivalence." *American Journal of Sociology* 92(6):1287–1335.

CAMBRE, M. A. 1981. "Historical Overview of Formative Evaluation of Instructional Media Products." *Educational Communications and Technology Journal* 29:3–25.

CAMPBELL, D. T., AND J. STANLEY. 1963. *Experimental and Quasi-Experimental Designs for Research*. Chicago: Rand McNally.

CARNOY, M. 1975. "The Economic Costs and Returns to Educational Television." *Economic Development and Cultural Change* 28:207–248.

CHAFFEE, S., AND C. ROSER. 1986. "Involvement and the Consistency of Knowledge, Attitudes and Behaviors." *Communication Research* 13(3):373–399.

CHAMPNESS, B., AND M. DEALBERDI. 1981. "Measuring Subjective Reactions to Teletext Page Design." Report to the National Science Foundation. New York: New York University Alternate Media Center.

CHARTERS, W. 1933. *Motion Pictures and Youth: A Summary*. New York: Macmillan.

CHEN, M. 1984. "Computers in the Lives of Our Children: Looking Back on a Generation of Television Research," in R. E. Rice and Associates (eds.), *The New Media: Communication, Research, and Technology*, pp. 269–286. Beverly Hills, Calif.: Sage.

CHRISTIANS, C., K. ROTZOLL, AND M. FACKLER. 1983. *Media Ethics: Cases and Moral Reasoning*. New York: Longman.

COMPAINE, B., ED. 1984. *Understanding New Media*. Boston: Ballinger.

CHRISTY, K. 1988. "New Communication Technologies: What the Researchers Are Doing." Bowling Green, Ohio: Bowling Green State University, School of Mass Communication. Paper presented at the International Communication Association, New Orleans, May.

COOK, T. 1985. "Post-Positivist Critical Multiplism," in L. Shotland and M. Mark eds., *Social Science and Social Policy*. pp. 21–62. Beverly Hills, Calif.: Sage.

COOK, T., AND D. CAMPBELL. 1979. *Quasi-Experimentation*. Chicago: Rand McNally.

CULNAN, M. 1984. "The Dimensions of Accessibility to Online Information: Implications for Implementing Office Automation Systems." *ACM Transactions on Office Automation Systems* 2(2):141–150.

———. 1985. "The Dimensions of Perceived Accessibility to Information: Implications for the Delivery of Information Systems and Services." *Journal of the American Society for Information Science* 5(36): 302–308.

CZITROM, D. J. 1982. *Media and the American Mind: From Morse to McLuhan*. Chapel Hill: University of North Carolina Press.

DANOWSKI, J. 1982. "Computer-Mediated Communication: A Network-Based Content Analysis Using a CBBS Conference," in M. Burgoon (ed.), *Communication Yearbook, Vol. 6*, pp. 905–924. Beverly Hills, Calif.: Sage.

———. 1987. "Organizational Infographics and Automated Auditing: Using Computers to Unobtrusively Gather as Well as Analyze Communication," in G. Goldhaber and G. Barnett (eds.), *Handbook of Organizational Communication*. Norwood, N.J.: Ablex.

DERVIN, B. 1981. "Mass Communicating: Changing Conceptions of the Audience," in R. E. Rice and W. J. Paisley (eds.), *Public Communication Campaigns*, pp. 71–88. Beverly Hills, Calif.: Sage.

DODDS, W. 1973. "An Application of the Bass Model in Long-Term New Product Forecasting." *Journal of Marketing Research* 10:309–311.

DORDICK, H. S., AND F. WILLIAMS. 1986. *Innovative Management Using Telecommunications*. New York: John Wiley & Sons.

DOZIER, D., AND R. F. RICE. 1984. "Rival Theories of Electronic Newsreading," in R. E. Rice and Associates (eds.), *The New Media: Communication, Research, and Technology*, pp. 83–128. Beverly Hills, Calif.: Sage.

DURLAK, J. 1987. "A Typology for Interactive Media," in M. McLaughlin (ed.), *Communication Yearbook, Vol. 10*, pp. 743–757. Beverly Hills, Calif.: Sage.

DUTTON, W. 1981. "The Rejection of an Innovation: The Political Environment of a Computer-Based Model." *Systems, Objectives and Solutions* 1:179–201.

DUTTON, W., J. BLUMLER, AND K. KRAEMER, EDS. 1987. *Wired Cities: Shaping the Future of Communications.* Boston: G. K. Hall.

DUTTON, W., AND R. MEADOW. 1987. "A Tolerance for Surveillance: American Public Opinion Concerning Privacy and Civil Liberties," in K. Levitan (ed.), *Government Infrastructures,* pp. 147–170. Westport, Conn.: Greenwood Press.

DUTTON, W., E. M. ROGERS, AND S. JUN. 1987. "Diffusion and Social Impacts of Personal Computers." *Communication Research* 14:219–250.

ELTON, M., AND J. CAREY. 1984. "Teletext for Public Information: Laboratory and Field Studies." *New Directions in Program Evaluation* 23:23–43.

ESKIN, G. 1985. "Tracking Advertising and Promotion Performance with Single-Source Data." *Journal of Advertising Research* 25(1):31–39.

ETTEMA, J. 1985. "Explaining Information System Use with System-Monitored vs. Self-reported Use Measures." *Public Opinion Quarterly* 49:381–387.

FAULES, DON. 1982. "The Use of Multi-Methods in the Organizational Setting." *Western Journal of Speech Communication* 46:150–161.

FEDERAL REGISTER. 1979. Wednesday, April 18, 1979; Part IV, "Belmont Report." Washington, D.C.: Department of Health, Education, and Welfare.

FINN, S. 1987. "Electoral Information Flow and Student's Information Processing: A Computerized Panel Study," in M. McLaughlin (ed.), *Communication Yearbook, Vol. 10,* pp. 517–532. Beverly Hills, Calif.: Sage.

FISCHER, C. S. 1985. "Studying Technology and Social Life," in M. Castells (ed.), *High Technology, Space, and Society.* Beverly Hills, Calif.: Sage.

———. 1986. "The Revolution in Rural Telephony, 1900–1920." *Journal of Social History* 21:5–26.

———. In press. "Touch Someone: The Telephone Industry Discovers Sociability, 1876–1940." *Technology and Culture.*

FISHBEIN, M., AND I. AJZEN. 1975. *Belief, Attitude, Intention and Behavior.* Reading, Mass.: Addison-Wesley.

FLAHERTY, D. 1985. *Protecting Privacy in Two-Way Electronic Services.* White Plains, N.Y.: Knowledge Industries.

FLAY, B. R., AND T. D. COOK. 1981. "Evaluation of Mass Media Prevention Campaigns," in R. E. Rice and W. J. Paisley (eds.), *Public Communication Campaigns,* pp. 239–268. Beverly Hills, Calif.: Sage.

FRANZ, C., AND D. ROBEY. 1986. "Organizational Context, User Involvement, and the Usefulness of Information Systems." *Decision Sciences* 17(3):329–357.

FREEDMAN, W. 1987. *The Right of Privacy in the Computer Age.* Westport, Conn.: Greenwood Press.

GALE, B. T. 1980. "Can More Capital Buy Higher Productivity?" *Harvard Business Review*, July–August.

GALLIERS, R. 1985. "In Search of a Paradigm for Information Systems Research," in E. Mumford, R. Hirschheim, G. Fitzgerald, and A. T. Wood-Harper (eds.), *Research Methods in Information Systems*, pp. 281–297. Amsterdam: Elsevier.

GEERTZ, C. 1973. *The Interpretation of Cultures: Selected Essays*. New York: Basic Books.

GITLIN, T. 1983. *Inside Prime Time*. New York: Pantheon.

GRANOVETTER, M. 1978. "Threshold Models of Collective Behavior." *American Journal of Sociology* 83:1420–1443.

————. 1982. "The Strength of Weak Ties: A Network Theory Revisisted," in P. Marsden and N. Lin (eds.), *Social Structure and Network Analysis*, pp. 105–130. Beverly Hills, Calif.: Sage.

GUTEK, B. 1982. "Effects of 'Office of the Future' Technology on Users: Results of a Longitudinal Field Study," in G. Mensch and R. J. Niehaus (eds.), *Work, Organizations and Technological Change*, pp. 191–212. New York: Plenum.

HABERMAS, J. 1984. *The Theory of Communicative Action: Vol. 1—Reason and the Rationalization of Society*. Translated by T. McCarthy. Boston: Beacon Press.

HART, P., AND R. E. RICE. 1988. "Interindustry Relations in Electronic New Services." *Journal of the American Society for Information Science*, in press.

HARTLEY, C., M. BRECHT, P. PAGEREY, G. WEEKS, A. CHAPANIS, AND D. HOECKER. 1977. "Subjective Time Estimates of Work Tasks by Office Workers." *Journal of Occupational Psychology* 50:23–36.

HIEMSTRA, G. 1982. "Teleconferencing, Concern for Face, and Organizational Culture," in M. Burgoon (ed.), *Communication Yearbook, Vol. 6*, pp. 874–904. Beverly Hills, Calif.: Sage.

————. 1983. "You Say You Want a Revolution? 'Information Technology' in Organizations," in R. Bostrom (ed.), *Communication Yearbook, Vol. 7*, pp. 802–827. Beverly Hills, Calif.: Sage.

HILTZ, S. R. 1979. "Using Computer Conferencing to Conduct Opinion Research." *Public Opinion Quarterly*, Winter, pp. 562–571.

————. 1982. "Experiments and Experiences with Computerized Conferencing," in R. Landau, J. Bair, and J. Siegman (eds.), *Emerging Office Systems*, pp. 182–204. Norwood, N.J.: Ablex.

HILTZ, S. R., AND M. TUROFF. 1981. "Evolution of User Behavior in a Computerized Conferencing System." *Communications of the ACM* 24(11):739–751.

HIRSCHHEIM, R. 1985. *Office Automation: A Social and Organizational Perspective*. New York: John Wiley & Sons.

HOLZER, M., AND A. HALACHMI, EDS. 1986. *Strategic Issues in Public Sector Productivity.* San Francisco: Jossey-Bass.

HOMANS, G. C. 1949. "The Strategy of Industrial Sociology." *American Journal of Sociology* 54(4):330–337.

HORTON, D., AND R. WOHL. 1956. "Mass Communication and Parasocial Interactions: Observations on Intimacy at a Distance." *Psychiatry* 19:215–229.

HOWARD, G., AND R. SMITH 1986. "Computer Anxiety in Management: Myth or Reality?" *Communications of the ACM* 29(7):611–615.

HUDSON, H. E. 1984. *When Telephones Reach the Village: The Role of Telecommunications in Rural Development.* Norwood, N.J.: Ablex.

HURT, H. T., K. JOSEPH, AND C. COOK. 1977. "Scales for the Measurement of Innovativeness." *Human Communication Research* 4(1):58–65.

HURT, H. T., AND C. W. TEIGEN. 1977. "The Development of a Measure of Perceived Organizational Innovativeness," in B. D. Ruben (ed.), *Communication Yearbook, Vol. 1*, pp. 377–85. New Brunswick, N.J.: Transactions Books.

IVES, B., M. OLSON, J. BAROUDI. 1983. "The Measurement of User Information Satisfaction." *Communications of the ACM* 26(10):785–793.

JARVANPAA, S., G. DICKSON, AND G. DESANCTIS. 1985. "Methodological Issues in Experimental IS Research: Experiences and Recommendations." *MIS Quarterly* 9(2):141–156.

JENKINS, A. M. 1985. "Research Methodologies and MIS Research," in E. Mumford, R. Hirschheim, G. Fitzgerald, and A. T. Wood-Harper (eds.), *Research Methods in Information Systems*, pp. 103–118. Amsterdam: Elsevier.

JICK, TODD. D. 1979. "Mixing Qualitative and Quantitative Methods: Triangulation in Action." *Administrative Science Quarterly* 24:602–611.

JOHANSEN, R., R. MILLER, AND J. VALLEE. 1974. "Group Communication Through Electronic Media: Fundamental Choices and Social Effects." *Educational Technology*, August 7–20.

JOHNSON, B., AND R. E. RICE. 1987. *Managing Organizational Innovation: The Evolution from Word Processing to Office Information Systems.* New York: Columbia University Press.

JONSCHER, C. 1985. "Assessing the Benefits of Telecommunications." *Intermedia*, January, pp. 21–24.

KATZ, E. 1962. "Notes on the Unit of Adoption in Diffusion Research." *Sociological Inquiry* 32:3–9.

KENDRICK, J. W., AND D. CREAMER. 1965. *Measuring Company Productivity: A Handbook with Case Studies in Business Economics*, No. 89. New York: National Industrial Conference Board.

KERLINGER, F. 1973. *Foundations of Behavioral Research*, 2nd ed. New York: Holt, Rinehart and Winston.

KERR, E. B., AND S. R. HILTZ. 1982. *Computer Mediated Communication Systems*. New York: Academic Press.

KERSTEN, A. 1986. "Philosophical Foundations for the Construction of Critical Knowledge," in M. McLaughlin (ed.), *Communication Yearbook*, Vol. 9, pp. 756–774. Beverly Hills, Calif.: Sage.

———. 1987. "Multilevel Analysis in Critical Research," in M. McLaughlin (ed.), *Communication Yearbook*, Vol. 10, pp. 709–726. Beverly Hills, Calif.: Sage.

KIESLER, S., AND L. SPROULL. 1986. "Response Effects in the Electronic Survey." *Public Opinion Quarterly* 50:402–413.

KISHCHUK, N., AND G. GURD. 1987. "Threats to Validity and Critical Multiplism in Social Research: The Case of Human Communications Technology Research." Paper presented at the International Communication Association, Montreal, May.

KLAPPER, J. 1960. *The Effects of Mass Communication*. New York: The Free Press.

KLOPFENSTEIN, B. 1986. "Forecasting the Market for New Communication Technology: The Home Video Player Experience." Paper presented at the International Communication Association, Chicago.

KNOKE, D., AND J. KUKLINSKI. 1982. *Network Analysis*. Beverly Hills, Calif.: Sage.

KRUGMAN, H. 1965. "The Impact of Television Advertising: Learning Without Involvement." *Public Opinion Quarterly* 29:349–356.

KUHN, T. S. 1970. *The Structure of Scientific Revolutions*. Chicago: University of Chicago Press.

LANCASTER, G. A., AND G. WRIGHT. 1983. "Forecasting the Future of Video Using a Diffusion Model." *European Journal of Marketing* 17:70–79.

LAROSE, R. 1980. "Formative Evaluation of Children's Television as Mass Communication Research," in B. Dervin and M. J. Voigt (eds.), *Progress in Communication Sciences*, Vol. 2, pp. 275–297. Norwood, N.J.: Ablex.

LATANE, B. 1987. "Social Science Should Invest in Infrastructure." *Social Science* 72(1):1–16.

LAZARSFELD, P., B. BERELSON, AND H. GAUDET. 1944. *The People's Choice*. New York: Columbia University Press.

LEIBERMAN, M. A., G. J. SELIG, AND J. J. WALSH. 1982. *Office Automation: A Manager's Guide for Improved Productivity*. New York: John Wiley & Sons.

LEVIN, H. M. 1983. *Cost Effectiveness: A Primer*. Beverly Hills, Calif.: Sage.

LOWERY, S., AND M. L. DEFLEUR. 1983. *Milestones in Mass Communication Research: Media Effects*. New York: Longman.

MAKRIDAKIS, S. AND M. HIBON. 1979. "Accuracy of Forecasting: An Empirical Investigation." *Journal of the Royal Statistical Society* 142:97–125.

MARKUS, M. L. 1987. "Toward a Critical Mass Theory of Interactive Media: Universal Access, Interdependence and Diffusion." *Communication Research* 14(5):491–511.

MAYER, R. N. 1986. "Videotex in France: The Other French Revolution." Working Paper 86-5. Salt Lake City: University of Utah Department of Family and Consumer Studies.

McCORMACK, T. 1986. "Reflections on the Lost Vision of Communication Theory," in S. J. Ball-Rokeach and M. G. Cantor (eds.), *Media, Audience, and Social Structure*, pp. 34–42. Beverly Hills, Calif.: Sage.

McGRATH, J. 1982. "Dilemmatics: The Study of Choices and Dilemmas," in J. McGrath, J. Martin, and R. Kulka (eds.), *Judgment Calls in Research*, pp. 69–102. Beverly Hills, Calif.: Sage.

McGUIRE, W. 1981. "Theoretical Foundations of Campaigns," in R. E. Rice and W. J. Paisley (eds.), *Public Communication Campaigns*, pp. 41–70. Beverly Hills, Calif.: Sage.

McLUHAN, M. 1964. *Understanding Media: The Extensions of Man*. New York: McGraw-Hill.

MIELKE, K. W., AND M. CHEN. 1983. "Formative research for '3-2-1 Contact,' Methods and Insights," in M. Howe (ed.), *Learning from Television*, pp. 31–55. London: Academic Press.

MISHAN, E. J. 1976. *Cost-Benefit Analysis*. New York: Praeger.

MITCHELL, J. C. 1969. "The Concept and Use of Social Networks," in J. C. Mitchell (ed.), *Social Networks in Urban Situations*, pp. 1–50. Manchester, Eng.: Manchester University Press.

MODY, B. 1985. "First World Communication Technologies in Third World Contexts," in E. M. Rogers and F. Balle (eds.), *The Media Revolution in America and in Western Europe*, pp. 134–140. Norwood, N.J.: Ablex.

MONGE, P. R., AND J. CAPELLA, EDS. 1980. *Multivariate Techniques in Human Communication Research*. New York: Academic Press.

MONGE, P. R., R. FARACE, K. MILLER, AND E. EISENBERG. 1984. "The Process of Studying Process in Organizational Communication." *Journal of Communication* 34:22–43.

MORGAN, G., ED. 1983. *Beyond Method*. Beverly Hills, Calif.: Sage.

MORITA, I. T., AND D. K. GAPEN 1977. "A Cost Analysis of the Ohio State Library Center On-Line Shared Cataloging System in the Ohio State University Libraries." *Library and Technical Service* 21(3):286–301.

MOSCO, V. 1982. *Pushbutton Fantasies: Critical Perspectives on Videotex and Information Technology*. Norwood, N.J.: Ablex.

MUMFORD, E., R. HIRSCHHEIM, G. FITZGERALD, AND A. T. WOOD-

HARPER, EDS. 1985. *Research Methods in Information Systems*. Amsterdam: Elsevier.

MUNDEL, M. E. 1983. "Work-Unit Analysis," in R. N. Lehrer (ed.), *White Collar Productivity*, pp. 201–233. New York: McGraw-Hill.

NEWSTED, P. 1985. "Paper versus On-Line Presentations of Subjective Questionnaires." *International Journal of Man-Machine Studies* 23:231–247.

OGAN, C. L. 1985. "Media Diversity and Communications Policy: Impact of VCR's and Satellite TV." *Telecommunications Policy* 9:63–73.

OLIVER, P., G. MAXWELL, AND R. TEIXEIRA. 1985. "A Theory of Critical Mass: Interdependence, Group Heterogeneity, and the Production of Collective Action." *American Journal of Sociology* 91:522–556.

OLSON, M. 1965. *The Logic of Collective Action: Public Goods and the Theory of Groups*. Cambridge, Mass.: Harvard University Press.

PAISLEY, W. J. 1984. "Communication in the Communication Sciences," in B. Dervin and M. J. Voigt (eds.), *Progress in the Communication Sciences*, Vol. 5, pp. 1–43. Norwood, N.J.: Ablex.

PALMER, E. L. 1974. "Formative Research in Production of Television for Children," in D. R. Olsen (ed.), *Media and Symbols: The Forms of Expression, Communication and Education*, pp. 303–329. Chicago: University of Illinois Press.

PARKER, E. B. 1973a. "Implications of New Information Technology." *Public Opinion Quarterly* 37:590–600.

———. 1973b. "Technological Change and the Mass Media," in I. Pool, W. Schramm, F. Frey, N. Maccoby, and E. Parker (eds), *Handbook of Communication*, pp. 619–645. Chicago: Rand McNally.

PARSONS, G. L. 1983. "Information Technology: A New Competitive Weapon." *Sloan Management Review*, 25.

PC MAGAZINE. 1986. "PC Advisor." *PC Magazine*, September 30, p. 27.

PETTY, R., AND J. CACIOPPO 1984. "The effects of Involvement on Responses to Argument Quantity and Quality: 'Central and Peripheral Routes to Persuasion." *Journal of Personality and Social Psychology* 46:69–81.

POOL, I. D. 1977. *The Social Impact of the Telephone*. Cambridge, Mass.: MIT Press.

———. 1983a. *Forecasting the Telephone: A Retrospective Technology Assessment*. Norwood, N.J.: Ablex.

———. 1983b. *Technologies of Freedom*. Cambridge, Mass.: Harvard University Press.

POOL, I. D. AND W. SCHRAMM, EDS. 1977. *Handbook of Communication*. Chicago: Rand McNally.

PUTNAM, L. 1983. "The Interpretive Perspective: An Alternative to Functionalism," in L. Putnam and M. Pacanowsky (eds.), *Communications and Organizations: An Interpretive Approach*, pp. 31–54. Beverly Hills, Calif.: Sage.

PUTNAM, L., AND M. PACANOWSKY, EDS. 1983. *Communications and Organizations: An Interpretive Approach*. Beverly Hills, Calif.: Sage.

RANDLES, F. 1983. "On the Diffusion of Computer Terminals in an Established Engineering Environment." *Management Science* 29(4):465–476.

REAGAN, J. 1987. "Classifying Adopters and Nonadopters of Four Technologies Using Political Activity, Media Use, and Demographic Variables." *Telematics and Informatics* 4:3–16.

REARDON, K. K. 1987. *Interpersonal Communication: Where Minds Meet*. Belmont, Calif.: Wadsworth.

REARDON, K. K., AND E. M. ROGERS. 1988. "Interpersonal versus Mass Media Communication: A False Dichotomy." *Human Communication Research*, in press.

REESE, S., P. SHOEMAKER, AND W. DANIELSON. 1987. "Social Correlates of Public Attitudes Toward New Communication Technologies." *Journalism Quarterly* 63(4):675–682.

RICE, R. E. 1982. "Communication Networking in Computer-Conferencing Systems: A Longitudinal Study of Group Roles and System Structure," in M. Burgoon (ed.), *Communication Yearbook, Vol. 6*, pp. 925–944. Beverly Hills, Calif.: Sage.

———. 1984. "Mediated Group Communication," in R. E. Rice and Associates (eds.), *The New Media: Communication, Research, and Technology*, pp. 129–154. Beverly Hills, Calif.: Sage.

———. 1987a. "Communication Technologies, Human Communication Networks and Social Structure in the Information Society," in J. Schement and L. Lievrouw (eds.), *Competing Visions, Complex Realities*, pp. 107–120. Norwood, N.J.: Ablex.

———. 1987b. "Computer-Mediated Communication Systems and Organizational Innovation." *Journal of Communication* 37:64–94.

———. 1988. "Issues and Concepts in Research on Computer-Mediated Communication Systems," in J. Anderson (ed.), *Communication Yearbook, Vol. 12*, in press. Beverly Hills, Calif.: Sage.

RICE, R. E., AND ASSOCIATES, EDS. 1984. *The New Media: Communication, Research, and Technology*. Beverly Hills, Calif.: Sage.

RICE, R. E., AND G. BARNETT. 1986. "Group Communication Networks in Electronic Space: Applying Metric Multidimensional Scaling," in M. McLaughlin (ed.), *Communication Yearbook, Vol. 9*, pp. 315–326. Beverly Hills, Calif.: Sage.

RICE, R. E., AND C. BORGMAN. 1983. "The Use of Computer-Monitored Data in Information Science and Communication Research." *Journal of the American Society for Information Science* 34:247–256.

RICE, R. E., A. GRANT, J. SCHMITZ, AND J. TOROBIN. 1988. "Critical Mass and Social Influence: A Network Approach to Predicting the Adoption, Use, and Outcomes of Electronic Messaging." *Communication Research*, in press.

RICE, R. E., AND LOVE, G. 1987. "Electronic Emotion: Socioemotional Content in a Computer-Mediated Communication Network." *Communication Research* 14:85–108.

RICE, R. E., AND W. J. PAISLEY. 1982. "The Green Thumb Videotext Experiment: Evaluation and Policy Implications." *Telecommunications Policy* 6(3):223–236.

RICE, R. E., AND W. RICHARDS, JR. 1985. "An Overview of Network Analysis Methods," in B. Dervin and M. Voigt (eds.), *Progress in Communication Sciences*, Vol. 6, pp. 105–165. Norwood, N.J.: Ablex.

RICE, R. E., AND E. M. ROGERS. 1980. "Re-Invention and Innovation: The Case of Dial-A-Ride." *Knowledge* 1(4):499–514.

RICE, R. E., AND D. SHOOK. 1988. "Access to and Usage of Integrated Office Systems: Implications for Organizational Communication." *ACM Transactions on Office Information Systems*, in press.

ROGERS, E. M. 1979. *Handbook of Formative Evaluation in Communication Design*. Stanford, Calif.: Stanford University, Institute for Communication Research.

———. 1983. *Diffusion of Innovations*. New York: The Free Press.

———. 1986. *Communication Technology: The New Media in Society*. New York: The Free Press.

ROGERS, E. M., AND D. L. KINCAID. 1981. *Communication Networks: A New Paradigm for Research*. New York: The Free Press.

ROSER, C. 1987. "Cognition and Affect in Persuasion: An Empirical Analysis of Involvement." Paper presented to the International Communication Association, Montreal, May.

ROWLAND, W. D., JR. 1982. *Politics of TV Violence*. Beverly Hills, Calif.: Sage.

———. 1986. "American Telecommunications Policy Research: Its Contradictory Origins and Influences." *Media, Culture and Society* 8:160–182.

RUBIN, A., E. PERSE, AND R. POWELL. 1985. "Loneliness, Parasocial Interaction, and Local Television News Viewing." *Human Communication Research* 12(2):155–180.

RYAN, B., AND N. C. GROSS. 1943. "The Diffusion of Hybrid Seed Corn in Two Iowa Communities." *Rural Sociology* 8:15–24.

SALMON, C. 1986. "Perpsectives on Involvement in Consumer and Communication Research," in B. Dervin and M. Voigt (eds.), *Progress in Communication Sciences*, Vol. 8, pp. 243–268. Norwood, N.J.: Ablex.

SASSONE, P. 1988. "Cost-Benefit Analysis of Information Systems: A Survey of Methodologies," in R. Allen (ed.), *Proceedings of the Conference on*

Office Information Systems. Washington, D.C.: Association for Computing Machinery, in press.

SCHILLER, H. 1982. *Who Knows? Information in the Age of the* Fortune *500.* Norwood, N.J.: Ablex.

SCHRAMM, W. n.d. "Notes on Case Studies of Instructional Media Projects." Working Paper. Washington, D.C.: Information Center on Instructional Technology, Academy for Educational Development.

———. 1985. "The Beginnings of Communication Study in the United States," in E. M. Rogers and F. Balle (eds.), *The Media Revolution in America and in Western Europe,* pp. 200–211. Norwood, N.J.: Ablex.

SCRIVEN, M. 1980. *Evaluation Thesaurus.* Point Reyes, Calif.: Edgepress.

SHANNON, C. E., AND W. WEAVER. 1949. *The Mathematical Theory of Communication.* Urbana: University of Illinois Press.

SHAW, M. 1978. "Communication Networks," in L. Berkowitz (ed.), *Group Processes,* pp. 313–349. New York: Academic Press.

SIEGEL, S., AND W. KAEMMERER. 1978. "Measuring the Perceived Support for Innovation in Organizations." *Journal of Applied Psychology* 63(5):553–562.

SLACK, J., AND F. FEJES, EDS. 1984. *The Ideology of the Information Society.* Norwood, N.J.: Ablex.

SMITH, M. J. 1988. *Contemporary Communication Research Methods.* Belmont, Calif.: Wadsworth.

SPROULL, L. 1986. "Using Electronic Mail for Data Collection in Organizational Research." *Academy of Management Journal* 29(1):159–169.

SPROULL, L., AND S. KIESLER. 1986. "Reducing Social Context Cues: Electronic Mail in Organizational Communication." *Management Science* 32:1492–1512.

STEINFIELD, C. 1983. "Communicating via Electronic Mail." Ph.D. thesis. Los Angeles: University of Southern California.

STEMPEL, G., III, AND B. WESTLEY. 1981. *Research Methods in Mass Communication.* Englewood Cliffs, N.J.: Prentice-Hall.

STONE, P., AND D. DUNPHY. 1966. "Trends and Issues in Content Analysis Research," in P. Stone, D. Dunphy, M. Smith, and D. Ogilvie (eds.), *The General Enquirer,* pp. 20–66. Cambridge, Mass.: MIT Press.

STRASSMAN, P. 1980. "The Office of the Future: Information Management for the New Age." *Technology Review,* December–January, pp. 54–65.

———. 1985. *Information Payoff: The Transformation of Work in the Electronic Age.* New York: The Free Press.

STREETER, T. 1987. "The Cable Fable Revisisted: Policy and the Making of Cable Television." *Critical Studies in Mass Communication* 4:174–200.

Time. 1987. "Can a System Keep a Secret?" *Time,* April 6, pp. 68–69.

TURN, R. 1985. "Privacy Protection," in M. Williams (ed.), *Annual Review of Information Science and Technology*, Vol. 20, pp. 27–50. White Plains, N.Y.: Knowledge Industries.

TUROFF, M. 1978. "Instructions for Conducting a Technology Forecasting and Assessment Workshop," in S. R. Hiltz and M. Turoff, *The Network Nation: Human Communication via Computer*, pp. 317–335. Reading, Mass.: Addison-Wesley.

VAN TASSEL, J. 1987. "Affect, Involvement, and Interactivity: Modifying Health Behavior Using the Interactive Videodisc." Ph.D. thesis. Los Angeles: University of Southern California.

VIDMAR, N., AND D. FLAHERTY. 1985. "Concern for Personal Privacy in an Electronic Age." *Journal of Communication*, Spring, pp. 91–103.

VITALARI, N. 1985. "The Need for Longitudinal Designs in the Study of Computing Environments," in E. Mumford, R. Hirschheim, G. Fitzgerald, and A. T. Wood-Harper (eds.), *Research Methods in Information Systems*, pp. 243–265. Amsterdam: Elsevier.

VITALARI, N., A. VENKATESH, AND K. GRONHAUG. 1985. "Computing in the Home: Shifts in the Time Allocation Patterns of Households." *Communications of the ACM* 28(5):512–522.

WARTELLA, E., AND B. REEVES. 1985. "Historical Trends in Research on Children and the Media: 1900–1960." *Journal of Communication* 35:118–133.

WEBB, E., D. CAMPBELL, R. SCHWARTZ, AND L. SECHREST. 1966. *Unobtrusive Measures: Nonreactive Research in the Social Sciences*. Chicago: Rand McNally.

WEISS, C. H. 1972. *Evaluating Action Programs: Readings in Social Action and Education*. Boston: Allyn and Bacon.

WELLMAN, B. 1983. "Network Analysis: Some Basic Principles," in R. Collins (ed.), *Sociological Theory 1983*, pp. 155–200. San Francisco: Jossey-Bass.

WESTIN, A., AND M. BAKER. 1972. *Databanks in a Free Society: Computers, Record-Keeping and Privacy*. New York: Quadrangle Books.

WHITE HOUSE CONFERENCE ON PRODUCTIVITY. 1983. "Report of the Preparatory Conference on Private Sector Initiatives: Information Worker Productivity." Washington, D.C.: U.S. Government Printing Office.

WHITNEY, C., AND J. ETTEMA. 1986. *Research on Media Organizations*. Beverly Hills, Calif.: Sage.

WIENER, N. 1948. *Cybernetics, or Control and Communication in the Animal and the Machine*. Cambridge, Mass.: Technology Press; New York: John Wiley & Sons.

———. 1950. *The Human Use of Human Beings*. Cambridge, Mass.: MIT Press.

WILLIAMS, F. In progress. *Computer-Assisted Writing Instruction–an Update.*

WILLIAMS, F., J. COULOMBE, AND L. LIEVROUW. 1983. "Children's Attitudes Toward Small Computers: A Preliminary Study." *Educational Communication and Technology* 31:3–7.

WILLIAMS, F., AND H. S. DORDICK. 1983. *The Executive's Guide to Information Technology.* New York: John Wiley & Sons.

WILLIAMS, F., R. LaROSE, AND F. FROST. 1981. *Children, Television and Sex-Role Stereotyping.* New York: Praeger.

WILLIAMS, F., R. E. RICE, AND H. DORDICK. 1985. "Behavioral Loci of the Information Society," in B. Ruben (ed.), *Information and Behavior, Vol. 1,* pp. 161–182. New Brunswick, N.J.: Transactions Books.

WILLIAMS, F., AND G. VAN WART. 1974. *Carrascolendas: Bilingual Education Through Television.* New York: Praeger.

WILLIAMS, F., AND V. WILLIAMS. 1984. *Microcomputers in Elementary Education.* Belmont, Calif.: Wadsworth.

―――. 1985. *Success with Educational Software.* New York: Praeger.

WIMMER, R., AND J. DOMINICK. 1987. *Mass Media Research: An Introduction.* Belmont, Calif.: Wadsworth.

WITHEY, M., R. DAFT, AND W. COOPER. 1983. "Measures of Perrow's Work Unit Technology: An Empirical Assessment and a New Scale." *Academy of Management Journal* 26(1):45–63.

YIN, R. K. 1984. *Case Study Research.* Beverly Hills, Calif.: Sage.

Index

Access, 60–61
Action research, 45–46
Albrecht, T. L., and Ropp, V. A., 50
Allen, R., 177
American Airlines, 157, 159–160
Anderson, J., and Jay, S., 167–168
Archival data, 94
Archival and secondary research, 36
Artificial intelligence (AI), 8
Asynchroneity, 13
Attention, 170
Attitude, 170, 172
Attitude scale construction research, 17
Audience response meters, 128

Ball-Rokeach, S. J., 173
Bass, F. M., 87
Behavior, 170, 172
Belmont Report, 178–179
Beniger, J., 174
Berger, C., and Roloff, M., 93
Bernard, H., 93
Bonoma, T., 39, 46
Booz Allen and Hamilton, 157
Boyd, D., and Straubhaar, J., 30
Bretz, R., 10

Cable television, 44, 83
Cambre, M. A., 119
Campbell, D. T., and Stanley, J., 58
Canonical correlation, 66
Capital-labor trade-off, 149
  example of, 156
Carey, John, 55–58
Carnoy, Martin, 134–137

"Carrascolendas," 123
Case study, 37–38, 66
  definition of, 107–108
  qualities of, 108–109
  steps for designing, 113–116
Case Study Research (Yin), 107
Cellular mobile telecommunications, 6
Census, 96
Central route of persuasion, 170
Chaffee, S., and Roser, C., 170, 171
Champness, B., and deAlberdi, M., 170
Charters, W., 25
Chen, M., 21, 85
Chicago School of Sociology, 32
Children, media and, 17, 18, 19–21
Children's Television Workshop, 117,
  119, 122
Chips; see Microprocessors
Christians, C., 186
Christy, K., 19
Cluster sampling, 64
Coaxial cable, 6
Code of Federal Regulations 45 CFR 46,
  "Protection of Human Subjects,"
  March 8, 1983, 179
Codes of research ethics, 177
Cohesion approach, 166, 167
Cohort study, 35, 65
Communication, 163
  levels of, 4
Communication effects, 25
Communication media, influence of, on
  research, 16
Communication Policy Act of 1984, Sec-
  tion 631, 185

Communication policy analysis, 27–28
Communication research, 3, 7
  direction of, 23–25
  history of, 16
Communication technologies, 4, 7
Communication theory, 21–24
Communications satellites, 6
Competitive advantage, 147, 157, 160
Computer Administered Panel Study
  (CAPS), 99
Computer bulletin board, 9, 97, 183
  example of adoption of, 75–77
Computer conferencing, 8, 9
Computer software copyright issues, 27
Computer-based health information sys-
  tems, adoption of, 167–168
Computerized card cataloging system,
  assessment of, 137–138
Computerized reservation system
  (Sabre), 157, 159–160
Computer-mediated communication, 9
Computer-monitored data, 91, 172
  characteristics of, 92–94
  examples of analysis of, 97
  merged with questionnaire data, 100–
  104
  types of, 95–97
  uses of, 94–97
Computer-monitored surveys, 98–99
Computers, 7–8, 17, 80, 163
Comte, Auguste, 38–39
Concept testing, 86
CONCOR, 167
Concurrent validity, 59
Consent form, 181–182
Construct validity, 59, 60
Content, 96
Content analysis, 37
Context, 25
Contextualism, 44–45
Control, definition of, 11
Conventional research, alternatives to,
  41–46
Convergence, 163, 164
Cook T., and Campbell, D., 58
Cost analysis
  applications of, 133
  examples of, 133–140
  steps in, 141–143
  types of, 132–133
Cost feasibility analysis, 133
Cost utility analysis, 132
Cost-benefit analysis, 131, 132, 133, 146
  example of, 153–154
Cost-effectiveness analysis, 132
Critical approach, 41, 42
Critical mass, 72–75, 77, 86
Cronbach's alpha, 61
Cross-case generalizations, 114

Cross-lagged correlation, 67
Cross-sectional studies, 64, 65
Culnan, M., 60
Cybernetic theory of communication,
  22–23
Cybernetics (Wiener), 22
Czitrom, D. J., 16

Danowski, J., 96, 185
Delphi method, 84–85
De-massification, 12–13
Dependent variables, 36
Deskilling, 150, 176
Dewey, John, 17
Diffusion, 72, 74
  definition of, 70
Diffusion curve, 81
Diffusion curve takeoff, 74, 75
Diffusion paradigm, 70–72
Diffusion research, 77–79
Digitalization, 7
Dislocation, 176
Disproportionate sampling, 64
Dodds, W., 87
Double-blind experiment, 33
Dozier, D., and Rice, R. F., 43, 170,
  173
Duration, 60, 95
Dutton, W., 65
Dutton, W., Blumler, J., and Kraemer,
  K., 66
Dutton, W., Rogers, E. M., and Jun,
  S., 88
Dynamic study, 65

Educational television, assessment of,
  133–137
Efficiency formula, 147–149, 159
Electronic messaging, 9, 75–77
Elton, Martin, 55–58
Equity, 150, 177, 185–186
Erie County Study, 98
Eskin, G., 93
Ethical guidelines, 179
Ethical issues, 176
Ethical principles, 178–179
"Ethics and New Media" (Communica-
  tions [1986]), 177
Ettema, J., 94
Evaluation, 126–127
Exchange of roles, definition of, 11
Experiments, 33
Expert judgment, 87
Exposure, 60, 95
External validity, 34, 56, 58–59, 62, 63,
  93, 96
Extrapolation, 85–86

Face validity, 59, 60
Face-to-face communication, 12
Factory analogy, 147
Faules, Don, 50
Feedback, 22–23
Field experiments, 34
Field studies, 35–36
Field trials, 56
Film, 17, 25
Finn, Seth, 99
Fischer, C. S., 29
Fishbein, M., and Ajzen, I., 130
Flay, B. R., and Cook, T. D., 123
Focus groups, 38, 86
Forcing quality, 74
Forecasting, methods of, 84–87
Forecasting research, centers of, 80–81
Forecasts, 79
  accuracy of, 81–83, 87
Formative data-gathering methods, 127
Formative evaluation, 117–119, 172
  characteristics of, 119–123
  as mass communications research, 129–130
  steps in, 124–129
  uses of, 123–124
Freedman, W., 184
"Freestyle," television project, 124, 127, 128
Frequency, 60, 95
Frequent flyer program (AAdvantage), 157, 159–160
Future of the Mass Audience Project, 80, 81
Futures research and forecasting, 36–37

Geertz, C., 43
Generalizability, 62, 121
Gitlin, T., 26
Granovetter, M., 75, 165
Group feedback analysis, 34
Gutek, B., 68

Hartley, C., 93
Hiemstra, G., 38, 43
High definition television, 9
Hiltz, S. R., 185
Hiltz S. R., and Turoff, M., 63, 65
Hirschheim, R., 44
Holzer, M., and Halachmi, A., 147
Horton, D., and Wohl, R., 173
Hotelling's T-square, 66
Hudson, H. E., 26
Human communication, 3
Human subjects, research with, 176, 177–181, 186
Human Use of Human Beings, The (Wiener), 22

Implementation, 118–119
Information Payoff (Strassmann), 152
Informed consent, 179
Initiator, 95
Innovation-decision process, 71
Innovations, 72, 75, 118
  adoption of, 70, 74, 78, 166
  attributes of, 71
  study of, 77–78
Innovativeness, 72, 78–79
Institute for the Future, 80, 83
Institutional General Assurance, 179–180
Integrated systems digital network (ISDN), 7
Intensity, 164
Interactive cable television, 9
Interactivity, 10–12, 23, 70, 163, 171–172, 174
  nature of, 169
Internal validity, 36, 56, 58, 59t, 62, 92
Interpretive approach
  characteristics of, 41
  principles of, 42
  processes of, 43
Intervening variables, 33
Involvement, 163, 169
Iran-*contra* affair, 181, 183

Jarvenpaa, S., 63
Jick, Todd D., 50
Johnson, B., and Rice, R. E., 47, 118, 133, 144
Jonscher, Charles, 139

Katz, E., 75
Kerr, E. B., and Hiltz, S. R., 60, 63
Kersten, A., 39, 40
Kiesler, S., and Sproull, L., 94
Klapper, J., 129
Klopfenstein, Bruce C., 79, 80, 87
Knoke, D., and Kuklinski, J., 166
Krugman, H., 169

Laboratory studies, 56
Lancaster, G. A., and Wright, G., 87
Larose, Robert, 122, 129–130
Latane, B., 104
Lazarsfeld, Paul F., 18, 98, 100
Learning, 171
Local area networks, 6
Logic of collective action, 73
Longitudinal studies, 35
Lowery, S., and DeFleur, M. L., 17, 18
Low-powered television, 9

Mainframe computer, 8
Makridakis, S., and Hibon, M., 87

Market analysis, 87
Markov analysis, 67
Markus, M. Lynne, 74
Mass communication research, 17-18
Mathematical modeling, 33
Mathematical theory of communication,
    22
McCormack, T., 23
McGuire, W., 171
McLuhan, Marshall, 28, 169
Media industry, structure of, 25-26
Media technology, study of, 28-30
MEDIACALC, 81, 85
Microcomputers, 8, 84, 85
Microcomputers in school
    example of case study of, 109-112
    study of, 106-108
Microprocessors (chips), 7
Microwave relay, 6
Mielke, K. W., and Chen, M., 123,
    127
Minitel system, 88-89
Mody, B., 45, 62
Monitor, 94-95
Morgan, G., 187
Morita, I. T., and Gapen, D. K., 137
Mosco, V., 43, 186
Mumford, E., 39
Mutual discourse, 10, 11

National Research Act (Public Law 93-
    348), 177, 179
Network analysis, 167
Network matrix, 164
Network paradigm, 164
Networks, 95-96, 163, 164
    analysis of, 166
    influence of, 166-168
New media
    definition of, 3
    special qualities of, 10-13
New media research, 13, 18-19
Newspapers, 17
Newsted, P., 94
Nielson or Arbitron ratings data, 91
Nuremberg Code, 178
N-way dimensional scaling, 67

Ogan, C. L., 30
Oliver, P., 73
Olson, Mancur, 73
One-way (linear) media model, 22-23,
    25
Operationalization, 60
Opportunity cost, 148
Optical transmission, 5
Over-time research, 64-65
    choices in, 65-66
    problems in, 67-78

Packet-switching, 6-7
Paisley, W. J., 24
Palmer, E. L., 117, 122
Panel study, 35, 65
Parasocial interaction, 173-174
Park, Robert E., 17, 32
Parker, Edwin B., 29, 83
Partial correlations, 66
Participant, definition of, 11
Participant observation, 37, 66
Payne Fund, 17, 25-26
People meter, 91
Peripheral route of persuasion, 171
Personal computers, 7, 92
    children's attitudes toward, 123
Petty, R., and Cacioppo, J., 170
Pilot project, 86
Pool, Ithiel de Sola, 26, 77, 83, 87
Pooled cross-sectional time-series, 35,
    65, 67
Positional approach, 166, 167
Positivism, 38-39
Positivist approach
    assumptions of, 38-39
    criticisms of, 39-40
Positivist research, 33-38
Predictive validity, 59
Pretesting, 120
Privacy, 177, 181, 183-185, 186
    computer data-bases and, 183-185
    in research, 185
Production ratios, 147-149
Productivity, 133, 146
PROFS (Professional Office System),
    100
Pseudo-communities, 174
Psychological involvement, 169, 170-
    172
Putnam, L., 42

Qualitative methods, 32
Quantitative methods, 32, 39
Quasi-experiments; see Field
    experiments
Questionnaires, 34-35, 94

Radio, 18
Randles, F., 65
Random sampling, 63
Randomness, 59
Rate of adoption, 72, 79, 81-83, 85
Reagan, J., 85
Real-time data, 95
Reardon, K. K., 16, 25
Reese, S., 184
Re-invention, 118
Relative-to-what concept, 134, 142
Reliability, 55, 56, 61, 64, 93

Repeated measures analysis of variance, 67
Research, vs. practice, 178
Research challenge, 14
Research designs
alternative, 13
elements of, 58–64
requirements of, 55
Research methods
conflict over, 32
criteria for choosing, 46–47, 48–49
Return-on-investment, 131
Return-on-investment ratios, 150
Revenue ratios, 149
Review boards, 180
Rice, R. E., 65, 67, 117, 163, 186
Rice, R. E., and Associates, 19, 25
Rice, R. E., and Barnett, G., 68
Rice, R. E., Grant, A., Schmitz, J., and Torobin, J., 75
Rice, R. E., and Love, G., 97
Rice, R. E., and Paisley, W. J., 185
Rice, R. E., and Richards, W., 166
Rice, R. E., and Shook, D., 60, 100
Risks and benefits, assessment of, 179, 186
Rogers, E. M., 16, 24, 70, 71, 86, 118, 121, 124
Rogers, E. M., and Kincaid, D. L., 166
Rowland, W. D., 16, 26
Rubin, A., 173

Salience, 170
Salmon, C., 170
Sampling, 55, 56, 62–64
Sassone, P., 131
Scales, 61
Schiller, H., 43, 186
Schramm, Wilbur, 16, 18, 107
Science of the practical, 3
Scriven, Michael, 117
Self-report data, 93–94, 100–102, 104
Service applications, 8–9
"Sesame Street," 117, 119, 122
Shannon, Claude E., and Weaver, W., 21–22
Shared tenant services, 6
Slack, J., and Fejes, F., 186
Social determinism, 24
Social involvement, 169
Social sciences, 24
Social system, definition of, 72
Sproull, L., and Kiesler, S., 76
Standardization, 28
Standardized regression coefficients, 66
Standards and variance analysis, 143–144
Statistical Analysis System, 102

Statistical methods, 66
Statistical prediction, 87
Steinfield, C., 124
Stone, Philip, 97
Stone, Philip, and Dunphy, D., 97
Strassmann, Paul, 152
Strategic investment, 157
Stratified sampling, 63
Streeter, T., 44
Subject selection, 179
Subjective meaning, 41, 43
Subjectivism, 25
Summative evaluation, 117, 121–122
Supercomputers, 8
Surveys, 34–35, 96

Technology, 3, 24
Telecommunications, 5–7
assessment of expanded, 138–141
Teleconferencing, 8
Telephone, 26–27, 83
Telephone service, deregulation of, 28
Teletext, 8, 11–12
Teletext advertising, 27
Teletext research, case study of, 55–58
Television, 18, 20–21, 26, 85, 169
Temporal study, 65
Third World, 45, 134–137
Third-order dependency, 10
"3-2-1 Contact," 122, 127
Time-series, 35, 67
Time-sharing, 8
Tipping point, 75
Triangulation, 13, 61, 84, 93, 94, 107, 115, 127, 129,
example of, 47, 49–50
t-test, 66
Turoff, M., 85
Type II error, 56

Understanding Media: The Extensions of Man (McLuhan), 28
Unit of analysis, 113–114
University-based research institute, 18
Use, 60–61, 95

Validity, 55, 56, 58–60, 61, 63, 64
Value-added analysis, 147
example of, 154–155
Value-added common carrier networks, 6
Value-added concept, 151–152
Value-added ratios, 150–151
Van Tassel, J., 117, 124, 126, 171
Variables, 33–34, 35
VCR, 30, 80, 81, 83
copying with, 27
Videodisc, 12, 117–118, 126, 171–172
Videodisc player, study of, 79–80

Videotext, 9, 11–12, 83–84, 88–89
Vidmar, N., and Flaherty, D., 184
Vitalari, N., 65, 88

Wartella, Ellen, and Reeves, Byron,
    16, 19–20, 26
Watergate case, 183
Webb, E., 50, 92, 108
Webber, Max, 41
Weiss, C. H., 122
Wellman, B., 78

Westin, A., and Baker, M., 184
Wiener, Norbert, 22–23
Williams, Frederick, 29, 125, 133
Williams, Frederick, Coulombe, J.,
    and Lievrouw, L., 123
Williams, Frederick, LaRose, R., and
    Frost, F., 123, 124
Williams, Frederick, and Williams, V.,
    106, 112

Yin, Robert K., 107, 114